SAILBOARDING

SAILBOARDING

BASIC AND ADVANCED TECHNIQUES

by Peter Brockhaus and
Ulrich Stanciu

translated by Barbara Webb

ADLARD COLES LIMITED
GRANADA PUBLISHING
London Toronto Sydney New York

Originally published in German under the title 'Windsurfing'. Original
edition © Nymphenberger Verlagshandlung GmbH, München 1976.

First published in Great Britain by Granada Publishing
in Adlard Coles Limited 1978.
Reprinted 1979
Second edition 1980

Granada Publishing Limited
Frogmore, St Albans, Herts AL2 2NF
and
3 Upper James Street, London W1R 4BP
Suite 405, 4th Floor, 866 United Nations Plaza, New York, NY 10017 USA
Q164 Queen Victoria Buildings, Sydney, NSW 2000, Australia
100 Skyway Avenue, Toronto, Ontario, Canada M9W 3A6
PO Box 84165, Greenside, 2034 Johannesburg, South Africa
61 Beach Road, Auckland, New Zealand.

ISBN 0 229 11651 5   post 1st ed 797·124 BRO

Typeset by Preface Ltd, Salisbury, Wilts
Printed and bound in Great Britain by
Fakenham Press Limited
Fakenham, Norfolk

Granada ®
Granada Publishing ®

List of Contents

Sailboarding — the Exciting Development of a New Sport

Beginners Always Get Wet

The people out for a walk stood on the bank and shook their heads in amusement. There, out on the water, was a young man on a strange board carrying a sail, trying desperately to get under way — but the mast kept falling down and the young man generally fell in too. Naturally this amused the onlookers enormously. Still, there was a fair amount of wind, and the watchers honestly had to admit that they would be quite unable to control such an extraordinary sailing device any better.

Three weeks later, on another fine and breezy day, the walkers again stood on the bank staring out over the water, but this time they were not laughing — they were fascinated. There was the same young man on his board speeding past them with effortless elegance, leaning out against the wind, his body suspended above the water while the spray splashed and glittered. He sailed straight on until he had passed a pier, tacked, and then whizzed back again.

The onlookers were amazed that sailboarding could be learnt as quickly as that.

Four years ago, when we stood on just such a sailing surfboard for the first time and, like the friend we have just described, frantically tried to keep our balance while we moved forward a couple of hundred yards over the water, we came to the conclusion that it was just like sailing, only much less steady.

Three weeks later, however, our ideas had changed completely. We had spent every spare moment on the water, and several times had rushed along in force 4 winds. Sailboarding fever had gripped us, and has not yet lost its hold. We have often asked ourselves why it is that sailboarding is so enthralling, so breathtakingly enjoyable? It could be due to the fact that it combines the basic elements of four different sports, skiing, surfing, sailing and water skiing. What is more both the sheer pleasure and the sporting aspect of all these four sports are enjoyed simultaneously.

To take skiing as an example: doing jet turns on a mogul-covered piste is very similar to surfing over the white breaking tops of waves in force 5 winds. Swings through deep powder snow on a sunny winter's day are as satisfying as planing over a sparkling mountain lake. In both sports it is the human being that is important while his apparatus, be it skis or surfboard, is only an aid. The two sports also share the advantage that you are not limited to a particular area. You can ski in any mountainous region where there is snow, just as you can sailboard on any water, whether it be an ocean or a reservoir. Skiers and board sailors do not need permanent moorings like sailors with large boats, nor are they restricted to certain waters as is often the case with water skiers. The initial outlay for gear is also very similar. A fully-equipped sailboard costs around £500 or $1000 (1980) which is comparable to the cost of good skiing equipment including safety bindings, boots and clothes. Thereafter sailboarding wins hands down. Skiers can tell many a tale about how much they have to pay out year after year for ski-lifts, whereas no further outlay is needed for sailboarding apart from the cost of travel to the area where you will sail. The wind is free and will remain so.

Another important consideration is that sailboards, like skis, are easy to transport on any car and to store in any garage. Furthermore they can be launched from any beach or bank and are rigged ready to sail in a few minutes. From then on all is enjoyment.

Sailboarding — it Only Takes Five Hours to Learn

All these factors have contributed to the rapid expansion in the last few years of the still very new sport of sailboarding. In 1972 there were 200 sailboards in Germany, where it caught on quickest, and now there are over 200,000. The USA follows in numbers with an equally rapid expansion centred on Marina del Rey, California, and even the cold waters of Britain have not stopped the spread of this very popular sport, which is administered there by the Royal Yachting Association. Australia, a natural growth area for sailboarding, already numbers over 2,000 enthusiasts with an organisation in Edgecliff, New South Wales. There are 100,000 in France. There are over 200 certified schools in the USA, about 100 in Britain and a nucleus of fifty or so in Australia (where there are nevertheless over 100 fleets, so the framework for rapid growth is there). In America the pupil is awarded a certificate which is graded according to the wind speed he or she is considered safe to cope with, and most countries run special courses for instructors based on a syllabus recommended by an organisation such as the International Windsurfing Schools; this usually requires a written as well as a practical test.

It should not, therefore, be difficult to find a conveniently situated school of proper instruction. Introductory courses are generally run at weekends, where as little as five hours of instruction will usually enable the beginner to skip the otherwise tedious (and sometimes bruising) period of self-instruction which can often take several weeks of trial and error. Pupils learn maintenance, techniques and how to steer the board, possibly with a session or two on a simulator to get the feel of it before trying the real thing on the water. They are also instructed about dangers and safety precautions. People who teach themselves board sailing often get into dangerous situations while they are still learning and may sail into areas reserved for swimmers or into shipping channels, thus causing collisions and possibly hurting people. Before starting on any course, it is advisable to check that the school of your choice is a member of a recognised organisation and uses a properly constituted method of instruction with official certificates of competency. In part 2 of this book we have

assembled the experience of champions and experts so that, once you have learnt how to sailboard, you can improve your style and technique.

How it All Began

Sailboarding is a very young sport. It was only invented in 1969 — where else could it be but in America. The computer expert Hoyle Schweitzer and his friend Jim Drake, both from California, were determined to make an old dream come true: they wanted to find some way of getting out beyond the breakers to the open sea with relatively little effort. When wave-riding in breaking surf — their principal sport

The inventor of the Windsurfer, Hoyle Schweitzer, and his wife Diana.

— they were both tired of always having to paddle laboriously out against the incoming breakers. Their aim was not to invent a new sporting device but merely to develop an aid for wave-riding. As is so often the case with a great invention, the pioneering of this new sport was pure chance.

Hoyle Schweitzer and Jim Drake were convinced that, somehow or other, their aid to surfing had to be driven by the wind but, if it was to be able to work out to seaward against the wind, it would have to be able to sail extremely efficiently. They studied old sailing books for months on end and tried out the strangest ideas, but the crux of the problem was that the methods of setting the sail were either too complicated or too primitive. They had worked out all the theory, but many problems arose when they started to put theory into practice. They knew from sailing that a boat could be steered by varying the position of the mast, but how was the mast to be supported, how was the sail to be extended and, above all, how would the surfer keep his balance — sitting, standing or lying down?

Many good sailors who climbed aboard the finished *Windsurfer* without any instruction condemned it as impossible to sail after hours of unsuccessful attempts. This shows clearly how much thought and practical effort the inventors had put into it. Today it is acknowledged on all sides that they have been very successful. They just made use of parts that were already being produced, a surfboard, a universal joint (familiar in the motor vehicle industry), together with a mast and a wishbone boom that had been used earlier in sailing vessels, and out of these they invented an entirely new sporting device. They were able to do without many of the parts that make up a normal sailing boat, stays and shrouds to support the mast in particular, and they did not use a rudder. The consequence was that an entirely new sailing technique had to be developed — sailboarding. A new sport was born and, later on, even sailing experts generously acknowledged it to be the only really original idea to appear in the sailing world during the last hundred years.

In spite of the fact that the technique is extremely simple, the sailing characteristics of the surfboards are superior to those of most dinghies and yachts. It is not only faster than almost all of them but is considerably safer to sail in heavy weather and high seas. The new creation was soon christened Windsurfer, and this name reminds us that the two inventors were basically surfers rather than sailors. Today, now that windsurfing is organized as a new branch of sailing, the word 'windsurfing' does not really describe the sport accurately because most beginners learn on inland waters, and the sport could better be described as board sailing. True surfing, or wave-riding, is no longer a major factor. The sport was called windsurfing simply because Hoyle Schweitzer and Jim Drake patented their apparatus under the name of Windsurfer.

Nowadays the term board sailing is used as an alternative and covers all types of sailing surfboards, including the Windsurfer. In this book Windsurfer with a capital 'W' refers to Hoyle Schweitzer's patented craft, the sport in general and its participants are referred to as board sailing and board sailors, whilst the equipment is known as a sailboard; we also use the word sailboarding from time to time, not least in the title, because this is what the Royal Yachting Association originally decided to call it, before they changed their minds.

European Sailboarding Pioneers

In the summer of 1971 news of sailboarding reached Europe and people took immediate action. For example, the Swedes Rutger Genberg and Per Fjaested flew to Los Angeles to take a closer look. Calle Schmidt from Germany ordered two Windsurfers for rapid delivery and was able to try them out for the first time in April 1972. He had managed to get the group of sand yacht sailors from St. Peter Ording interested in this venture, and they included Uwe Schröder and Rüdiger Grassy who were world sand yacht champions. After two hours of battling in a muddy channel off St. Peter a bet was made. If Calle was able to master the recalcitrant beast and could make it alter course on the Alster in Hamburg by the following weekend, he would win a case of *Sekt*. Calle did not give up and won the bet. He had come to the conclusion that the invention was really worthwhile.

The first German sailboarding club was founded by Peter Raatz in Berlin on the Wannsee. Then the West German board sailors pressed the Deutscher Seglerverband hard to permit the formation of a Windsurfer Class. On Lake Constance the world's first sailboarding school was started.

It must be admitted that, because most beginners kept falling in repeatedly during their first hours of laborious efforts before they finally succeeded in making their first unsteady tack, the general opinion was formed that this was very much a specialist sport and far too difficult for the general public. This view was reinforced by German press reports which soon promoted the 'daring young men on their ironing boards' to super sportsmen.

The opposite proved to be the case. We were all ordinary people, looking for a sport that we could enjoy competitively in our brief leisure hours, and that would give us physical exercise.

The first sailboards arrived in Britain in 1973, but it was a year or two before the sport attracted much publicity and interest. In 1979 Prince Charles began windsurfing, and that same year saw almost 250 board sailors attend the National Championships at Hayling Island. Several associations have been formed to help promote the sport, which is overseen by the Royal Yachting Association. The RYA have set up a training programme to ensure a high standard of instruction at all windsurfing schools.

(Photo — Yachting World)

Derk, Bep and Wim Thijs exercise their three-man sailboard at the sailing speed trials at Weymouth, England.

The Start of Racing

The third decisive factor in the history of sailboarding was racing. In September 1972 the first European sailboarding regatta took place at Sylt in Germany. Calle Schmidt invited the enthusiasts, and they all came. The victor was Calle himself — how could it be otherwise. He had spent the entire summer concentrating on sailboarding and he set the standard. In those autumn days, with winds of force 4 to 5, about 30 competitiors tried to sail round a triangular course. Only a few succeeded because the wind was too strong for them, but a mere six months later, at Whitsun 1973, things were very different. A field of 50 surfers started and Calle was no longer alone in the lead. Werner Schulz from Eckernförde was the star of the year, and names such as Hein Schombara, Fritz Stiehl and Uwe Mahn Bartholme also figured in the list of winners.

A great deal of training was taking place in other countries too because the first European championships were to take place in September 1973. They were again held in Sylt and were a great event attracting no less than 160 starters. The European championship was won by a Dutch boy,

Derk Thijs, then fifteen years old, and he subsequently retained his title to show it was no chance win.

In Germany classes were established and racing organized in 1974. A few words of explanation are needed here for those who are not already involved in sailing. In the sailing world, as in motor racing, only boats of the same size, sail area and construction may compete against each other and boats are therefore divided into classes. Some of these sailing classes are restricted only as to certain measurements such as hull, sail, mast etc. but there are also one design classes built by specific manufacturers and controlled by rules which lay down strictly that a boat may only take part in a race in the same condition as that in which it was delivered by the yard. The yard is committed to building identical boats and to make no changes over the years. The advantage of these strict one design classes lies in the fact that the race is not won by the boat that has the best equipment and that has been best designed, but by the best sailor.

The Windsurfer, Windglider and Mistral have all been granted International Class status by the International Yacht Racing Union, and it seems certain that the sport will be accepted into the Olympics. Although there are few European one design classes

with such strict class rules it is evident that more and more sailors are being attracted to them because the cost of competing in restricted classes is so much higher. The 'racing machines' become ever more complicated and expensive, and a weekend sailor using a normal boat has no chance of winning a race. Even one of the most successful sailors in a class will not be near the front of the fleet when sailing a normal boat.

The arguments of those who dispute the merits of strict one design classes are also valid in that technical improvement is impossible due to the tight control of the rules. For example, when making tests, the team from the German magazine *Windsurfing* established that the mast foot of the Windsurfer does not function perfectly, and that the groove in the Windglider can cause injury in a fall, but these faults could not be remedied by the manufacturer until approved by the class association.

Racing men, however, are always trying to improve their sailing surfboards, for example by using better sails which they often have especially cut by well-known (and expensive) sailmakers, so as to gain even a slight increase in speed when racing.

Racing Progress

After Windsurfer class organizations had been established in all major continental countries in 1974, and an increasing number of races had been sailed, the second European championships were held in June 1974 in La Ciotat, Côte d'Azur, and showed what enormous progress had been made in this new sport. For example surfboards were now being sailed in winds up to force 8. Derk Thijs again clearly led the field and Hoyle Schweitzer, invited to compete by the organizers, proved with his second place that he had not only invented the Windsurfer but had mastered it. Third place went to the best German, Rainer Gutjahr.

The high point of 1974 was, however, the World Championships in the USA where, at the Association Island sailing club, about 30 Europeans met strong American competition for the first time. The European team was a strong one, with the two Thijs brothers from the Netherlands, Helgo Lass, Wille Schalge, Ludwig Graf von Seyssel from Germany and Yves Loisance from France.

The Europeans were outclassed in the very light winds which prevailed throughout the week. Only Derk Thijs made good to some extent, finishing in fifth place, while the rest were left well behind. The clear victors were the fourteen-year-old Matt Schweitzer, son of the inventor of the Windsurfer, and his friend Mike Waltze who was the same age. Third place went to the 1973 World Champion Bruce Mattlack. The general feeling among the Europeans after this meeting was 'just wait until these American flyweights race in heavier winds'.

A year later, in the World Championships in Bendor, Côte d'Azur, the Europeans were rubbing their hands with glee because it was blowing hard. For the first time in the history of this young sport the entire élite of the windsurfing world had gathered together. The American class association had sent its best men and women to Europe, while the Europeans were determined to take the title on this occasion. The wind was suitably strong and on some days even reached force 9 to 10. It was the moment for the heavy weather experts. Derk Thijs, Helgo Lass, Michael Buddeberg, Heini Müller and Ernstfried Prade were the crack surfers with the confidence to sail in such weather, and they gave a non-stop show before the races. The Americans were hardly to be seen on the water — they had not expected winds like this.

After the eliminating races, which were held in light breezes, the mistral returned as ordered for the finals. The best 60 men and 20 women windsurfers in the world started in separate races, while the wind blew between force 4 and 6 Beaufort scale, with gusts reaching force 7. This was a test which could hardly have been bettered. Sailing skill alone was decisive and no-one could complain of too little or too much wind.

The European strong wind experts had been gloating too soon, however, for these World Championships proved clearly that the best windsurfers still came from the USA. Lightweight Matt Schweitzer, now 15 years old, again became the champion, followed by Bruce Mattlack, Doug Halsey and Brian Tulley. The first of the Europeans, the Norwegian Thor Bakke, was fifth while Rainer Gutjahr, Derk Thijs and Ernstfried Prade finished seventh, eighth and ninth. They had shone in the show surfing, it is true, but they were completely outpaced when racing over the Olympic triangular course that was used.

The 1976 World Championships in Nassau in the Bahamas confirmed this result. The lightest competitor, the 13-year-old, 6 stone (84 lbs) Robby Naish from Hawaii won the world title, while the previous year's winner, Matt Schweitzer, took second place. The best German, Peter Kleinwächter, ended up ninth. Although the 1976 Championships were held in very light winds which inevitably gave the lightweights an advantage, an important fact has been proved by this series of World Championships. Sailboarding is not so much a sport for strong men as one which demands perfect technique, great skill and good physical coordination.

The Europeans returned home having learnt this lesson, and what they saw and learnt in the championships is very relevant for every sailboarder who is ambitious to do well in his new sport. Good style with an easy, relaxed stance, perfect technique when altering course, and regular training are the basic requirements for good sailboarders. Names appearing in British championships include Ken and Gordon Way, Graeme Fuller, Lisa Vincent, Mike Todd, John Hogarth, Peter Caldwell, Fiona McKay, and Ade White, with others snapping on their heels.

The Other Sailing Surfboards

Of other sailboards, the Mistral Surfer has earned a reputation for high quality, and was the first mass-produced sailboard to include a swivel dagger-board. A similar reputation is enjoyed by the HiFly which is easily recognised by its distinctive hull shape, a feature that leads to improved performance in light winds. This radical change in hull shape was inspired by Gary Seamen, who was the first to incorporate chines in sailboard hull design when he produced the sleek TC39. Several modern boards have followed his example, and not without success. The latest designs from Mistral, Windglider and Tornado are all characterised by a dinghy-shaped hull and, in their first competitive season, they took the first three places respectively in the World Open Class championships in Guadeloupe.

Most board manufacturers regard Open Class races (where different makes of board compete against one another) as their 'shop front', though one other event figures prominently in their thinking: the World Sailing Speed Record week held annually at Weymouth in the South of England. In October 1977 flying Dutchman Derk Thijs established a record of 19.1 knots on a Windglider; this was all the more remarkable in view of the fact that Thijs's 6.9 sq metre sail was well below the maximum of 10 sq metres

permitted in his class. Two years later the 'father' of British board sailing, Clive Colenso, took his Olympic Gold through the 500 metre course at a fantastic 22.9 knots — in a force 8 wind! Many of the world's best board sailors will continue to congregate at this annual event determined to beat that record.

But other records are being made too. In 1979 Britain's Mike Todd and Graeme Fuller crossed the English Channel in 3hr 23mins on a modified Windglider tandem using Alpha sails and Needlespar masts, to become the first holders of the Heineken trophy for the fastest crossing. A Ten Cate TC39 was sailed across the Bering Strait from Alaska to Russia by a Frenchman; this was the board which won the 1979 British championships, also sponsored by Heineken, thus proving that it can reach parts which others boards cannot reach. Another Frenchman, Frederic Beauchene, achieved the sensational feat of sailing round Cape Horn on a Dufour Wing. There are now special boards with foils, cathedral hulls and wing masts (with which Ken Way has achieved an unconfirmed 25 knots). There are even unwieldy four-man boards.

In Britain the most popular boards include Dufour Wing, HiFly, Sailboard, Olympic Gold, and the Sea Panther. These last two boards both use trapezium shaped booms made of light alloy, which are stiff, thus ensuring a good sail shape, yet comfortable to use. The shape of the boards and the material of which the booms and masts are made are not all the same, while the mast joints and their anchorages merely follow a common principle. The reader should not expect to find a complete review of the market here, but once he understands how the major parts of a sailboard function, he should judge for himself which product pleases him best. In this book we have concentrated largely on describing the Windsurfer and the Windglider because these are by far the most

widely distributed in Europe. It is important that your choice should not be based on what looks best but on the result of tests and trials. Later on you will sail your surfboard in conditions which you cannot imagine possible as a beginner. This is why your decision as to which surfboard to buy should be based on as much experience and expert knowledge as possible.

World champion Matt Schweitzer reaching with his daggerboard half raised.

Part 1

Basic Techniques

The Sailboard and its Component Parts

When constructing sailboards the manufacturers' main concern was to create simple, uncomplicated sporting craft which would be easy to handle and give maximum enjoyment. Their aim was not to build refined machines, and they therefore tried to keep the individual components of the surfboards as simple and basic as possible. For the most part they succeeded. The sailboard is quite unsophisticated, easy to assemble and handle, and light to transport. Furthermore all the parts are made of the strongest materials which resist wear and tear. There is nothing that will break quickly provided you look after it properly. In any case, correct handling and assembly are absolutely essential if you are to learn board sailing correctly.

First, therefore, you must learn the right way to rig and de-rig the sailboard, not least because your safety on the water depends on this. Consequently you must become familiar with the individual parts.

A sailboard with all its parts — there are only seven in all.

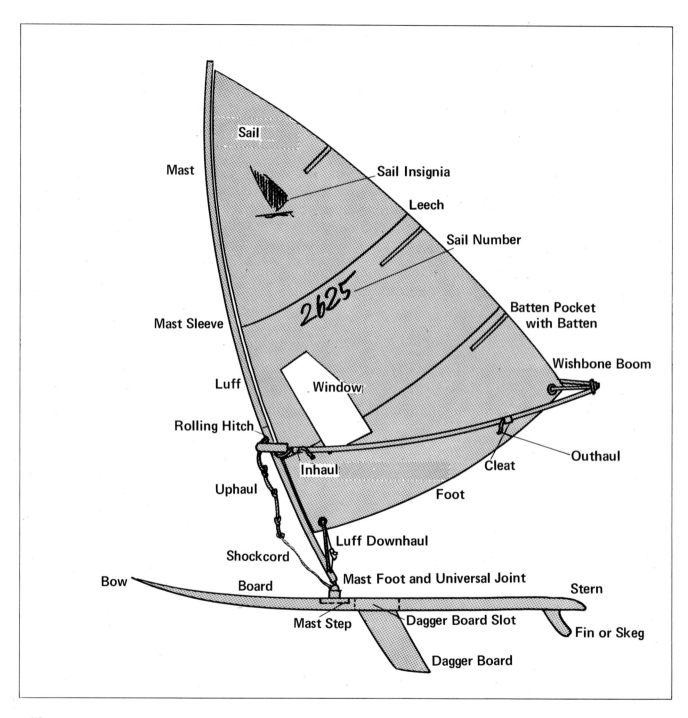

Sail

Mast

Sail Insignia

Leech

Sail Number

Mast Sleeve

Batten Pocket
with Batten

Luff

Wishbone Boom

Window

Rolling Hitch

Inhaul

Outhaul

Cleat

Uphaul

Foot

Luff Downhaul

Shockcord

Mast Foot and Universal Joint

Bow

Board

Stern

Mast Step

Dagger Board Slot

Fin or Skeg

Dagger Board

2625

The Board

Most sailboards are about 12ft 0in long and 2ft 3in broad. Depending on the manufacturer they are made either of polyethylene or fibreglass, filled with polyurethane foam. Therefore the board is made basically of plastics and this means that there are no problems over maintenance. Nor is the material affected by warmth, cold or salt water. The most important point is that *the board can never sink*. Even if it is holed water cannot enter because of the rigid foam inside, and it follows that the board is extremely safe. Later on, if you should get into difficulties on the water, stay on your board. It cannot sink and will keep you above water.

Transporting the board is easy enough too. It weighs about 40 lbs and can easily be carried under one arm by holding on to the daggerboard case. This is a slot in the middle of the board through which the daggerboard is pushed.

The Daggerboard

This is a specially moulded fibreglass or wooden flat board which is pushed down to discourage the surfboard from moving sideways through the water. It also ensures that the board will move straight ahead. When the surfboard is being transported the daggerboard can easily be pulled upwards out of the slot by the strap or line attached to it. Take care: when you are sailing in shallow water pull up the daggerboard in good time! If you run aground when it is down you could damage both the daggerboard and the slot. If you have a pivot in the system, the problem will not arise because the projection will hinge away automatically on striking the ground.

The Fin or Skeg

This is fitted under the stern of the sailboard and, like the fin of a water ski, serves to keep the sailboard on course and moving straight ahead. Some skegs are fastened permanently to the board (like the flexible plastic one of the Windglider), some are screwed on (like that of the Windsurfer), while some are neither screwed nor permanent, but can be easily removed for transport by pulling out, such as is the case with the HiFly.

The Mast Foot

The flexible joint at the lower end of the mast (see photo on p. 24) is the vital feature of the sailboard and enables the mast and sail to be turned and inclined in any direction desired. As you will soon find out, this is the reason why the sailboard can be steered so simply and accurately. Check whether the mast foot can be released easily, but not unintentionally, from the board if needed. Check too that the mast foot can be made fast to the hull; this is an important safety feature recommended by the RYA.

The Mast

The mast is a tapered, flexible and very light fibreglass or alloy tube, 13ft 9in long. It fits over the mast foot. Note that, whereas the Windsurfer's mast is connected to the foot in such a way that it can always be pulled out, the Windglider's mast foot is constructed somewhat differently and the mast and mast foot are fastened firmly together. The Windsurfer also has a short round wooden plug which has to be pushed into the upper end of the mast. This is the mast top and it has to be taped on to prevent water running into the mast.

The mast is subjected to great forces, especially in stronger winds. Handle it carefully and take care that the top and bottom ends in particular do not get bumped when it is being transported.

The Wishbone Boom

The wishbone boom has been designed especially for the Windsurfer and, depending on the manufacturers, is made of either laminated teak or alloy. At the forward end a stainless steel or fibreglass W-shaped bracket connects the two arms of the boom. This part of the wishbone boom is attached to the mast with a line called the inhaul as its job indicates. The uphaul line is also made fast here and is used to pull the sail up from the water. Several equidistant knots should be tied in this uphaul so that your hands will not slip when you are raising the rig. The uppermost knot will be a hand's span below the wishbone boom, while the lowest is at the lower end of the uphaul. The outhaul line is attached to the aft end of the wishbone boom and is used to tension the sail, the outhaul being made fast on a cleat fixed on one side of the boom.

If your boom has no handgrip you should wind good quality adhesive tape around it at the places where you will hold onto it when you are sailing, that is, 4—8in aft of the mast for the forward or mast hand, and about 20in further aft for the aft or sail hand. This tape should be applied before your first sail, and will give you a better grip. Your hands will not slip so easily, especially when they are under a heavy load. When strapping on the tape for the forward handhold start from aft and work forward, while for the aft handhold start from forward and work aft.

This will prevent the tape working free later when you are pulling sideways hard. Use green tape for the right hand half of the wishbone boom when looking forward, and red tape for the left hand side. You will see why later when you read the section on the rules of the road.

The Sail

The sail is a triangle about 60 sq. ft. in area, made of strong but very light synthetic material. The three edges of the sail are named as follows: luff, the forward edge; leech, the after edge; and foot, the bottom edge. The luff of the sail is also the mast sleeve, or luff sleeve, and the mast is pushed into it. There is a gap in the sleeve at the point where the wishbone boom is attached to the mast. At the lower end of the luff there is a metal eye in the sail. A line is led through this and connects the sail to the mast foot. This line is called the luff downhaul.

At right angles to the leech three narrow pockets are sewn onto the sail and the battens are pushed into

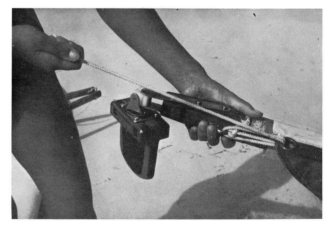
The luff downhaul attaches the sail to the mast foot.

them. They serve to maintain the convex curve of the leech.

Some sails incorporate a pocket near the foot. This can be used as a small stowage locker for money in a plastic bag, an extra line or other items (see photo on this page).

The sail is virtually the engine of the sailboard and, naturally, there are many tricks and dodges which enable you to make the best use of this engine. The subject of fine adjustment to the shape of the sail will be discussed fully later. The most important point is that you must look after the sail properly. Water does not harm it, but nevertheless a sail should be spread out to dry when it is wet or damp, because otherwise unsightly black spots of mildew will appear. Sails made of synthetic materials dry very quickly, but if you do not have time to dry yours immediately after it has been used, hang it up on the washing line at home. It is important too that you fold the sail carefully when storing it so that it does not lose its shape. The best method is to fold it in half, keeping the leech straight while the luff makes a zig-zag line. Then fold it across four times and it will stow neatly in the sail bag without becoming crumpled or going out of shape. Take care that the window or windows are not too sharply folded because this could cause the plastic sheet to break.

Another point: after using the sail for some time you may notice that the stitching of the seams is beginning to wear or fail in places. Repair the damage immediately with a needle and terylene thread because if you do not do so there is a danger that the whole seam will rip in stronger winds.

One of the best ways to take care of your sail is by using a mast/sail sock. In this method the sail remains on the mast and is rolled around it, before being sleeved by a long bag. This avoids any problems of creasing sail-cloth or windows.

Rigging the Sailboard

The next step is to assemble the various individual parts, in other words, to rig the sailboard. When you have practised this several times you will find that it can be done very easily in less than five minutes.

- In the case of the Windsurfer, first screw on the skeg so that it curves back towards the stern of the sailboard.
- Attach the mast top to the mast.
  — Slide the mast into the mast sleeve of the sail.
- Feed the sail battens into the batten pockets.
- Lead the luff downhaul through the lower eye in the sail near the mast sleeve and make it fast to the mast foot using a reef knot or several *half hitches*.

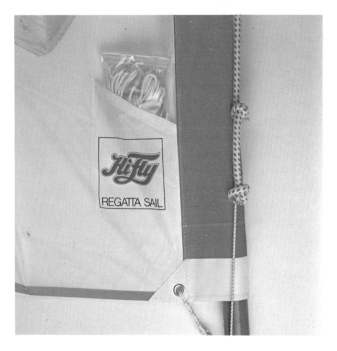

Pocket at the tack of a sail, for stowing safety line, money etc.

The bowline is one of the most useful sailors' knots. It makes a loop which will not slip, and can be undone even after being under great load. You use it to attach the outhaul to the end of the boom.

- Attach the wishbone to the mast. To do this you tie a *rolling hitch* round the mast with the inhaul at the point where there is a gap in the mast sleeve. The inhaul is then led through the eye at the forward end of the wishbone boom, hauled taut, and made fast to a cleat fixed to the side of the boom. Some boards have other systems. The HiFly's mast and boom clip together at any height on the mast (see photo on p. 28), whilst the Klepper's boom separates at the front end to clip round the mast.

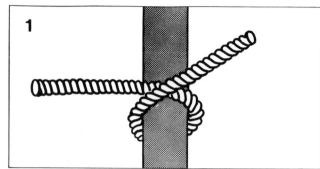

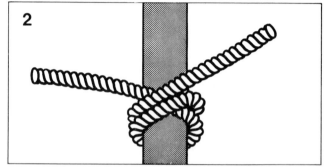

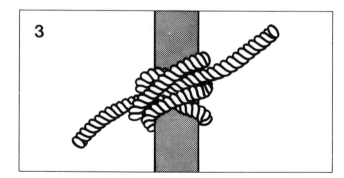

The rolling hitch is used to tie the inhaul or boom end line around the mast. It prevents the boom slipping down the mast.

This is how the mast foot is slipped into the mast. Make sure that both parts can turn independently.

- The outhaul is attached to the aft end of the boom by a *bowline*, and is then led through the after eye in the sail, back over the end of the boom, and made fast to the cleat on the side.
- There should be a piece of thin shock cord connecting the lower end of the uphaul to the mast foot so that later, when the sail is lying on the water, the uphaul is always ready at hand.

The battens are slid into the batten pockets. Be careful not to drop them into the water because they do not float.

The mast is pushed into the sleeve of the sail.

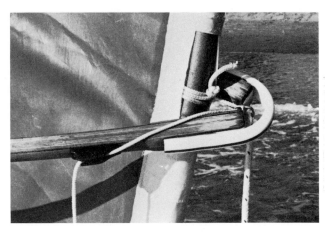

The boom should be tied tight against the mast like this.

You use the outhaul to pull the sail out to the end of the wishbone boom.

The final step when rigging the board; the mast foot is pushed into the mast step.

The rig is always carried to the water with the mast nearer to the wind.

- Take the rig, that is the mast, sail and boom, down to the water, and be sure always to carry it with the mast nearest to the wind. Place the rig in the water. It will float but not blow away.
- Only then will you carry your sailboard into thigh deep water and insert the daggerboard.

- Now push the mast foot into the board. If the mast foot of a Windsurfer fits too loosely, wrap good quality tape round it until it fits snugly. You should make sure, however, that you are able to pull out the mast foot at any moment without too much effort.

After these preparations have been made your sailing sailboard is ready.

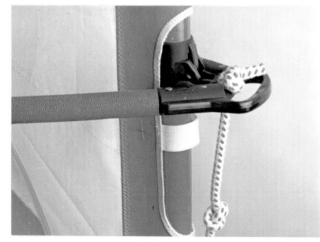

Mast/boom connection, adjustable in height.

Before Your First Attempt

The Wind

Before you climb onto your sailboard you should obviously know how and why everything works. The theory on which the sport is based is concerned above all with the motive power of the sailboard, namely the wind. When you are learning the most important rule to remember is that you must always know from which direction the wind is blowing. How can this be established? Quite easily. Pick up a few blades of grass and throw them into the air. You will soon see from which direction the wind is blowing. Alternatively you can lick one finger and hold it up: the wind comes from the side which feels coldest. You can also look at the trees which bend to the wind, or the little flags (burgees) at the tops of the masts of other sailing boats nearby, or at flags on land — they will all show you the wind direction.

It is extremely important to remember from which direction the wind is blowing. Later, when you are alone with your sailboard on the water, you must know where it is coming from at all times. The best way of finding the wind direction is by looking at your own shaking sail. Broadly speaking you have to consider three possible situations with regard to wind direction:

- Wind which is blowing parallel to the bank or shore, whether from the left or the right.
- Wind which is blowing from the land to the water — an offshore wind.
- Wind which is blowing from the water to the land — an onshore wind.

Even when you are not going sailboarding you should keep an eye open and check the trees and flags. You will then learn to recognize the wind direction automatically. You will develop a feeling for the wind and be aware of its direction almost instinctively.

And now a few words about the strength of the wind. Your first attempts at sailboarding must be made in light breezes which are no more than force 3 according to the Beaufort Wind Scale.

Force 1 — light air, the water is smooth or slightly rippled: wind speed 1—3 knots

Force 2 — light breeze, the water is rippled or with small wavelets: wind speed 4—6 knots

Force 3 — gentle breeze, large wavelets: wind speed 7—10 knots

The wind which you feel when you are standing on the bank is called the true wind. Why? Because there are two other winds that affect you when you are sailboarding. To make this clear just imagine that you are cycling on a day when there is no wind at all. In spite of the calm you will feel a breeze due to the speed of the bicycle. When a surfboard sails forward there will also be a wind caused by its forward motion, and the strength of that wind depends on the speed of the surfboard through the water. The sailboard's sail is affected by the true wind and by sailboard speed. Naturally these cannot be separated from each other when the sailboard sails forward, and when they are combined they are called the apparent wind.

IMPORTANT: It is always the apparent wind that is used when sailing.

When you are sailing dead before the wind, that is with the wind blowing directly over the stern, the direction of the wind due to sailboard speed is exactly opposite that of the true wind, and consequently the speed of the true wind is reduced by the surfboard's speed. On the other hand, when you are sailing with the wind abeam, in which case the true wind comes from the side while the wind due to sailboard speed comes, as always, from ahead, the apparent wind which is a combination of the other two winds will blow from a direction somewhere between them. The faster the sailboard sails, the further forward will be the direction of the apparent wind. This can best be understood by looking at the funnel of a large vessel. When the wind is abeam, the faster the vessel steams the further aft the smoke will be blown.

Theory

But the question remains — why does a sailboard sail forwards in spite of the fact that the wind often blows from the side or even at an angle from ahead?

With a following wind, that is, when the wind is blowing from aft, it is easy to explain that the sailboard moves forwards because the wind blows it ahead like a leaf. The sail brakes the wind and forward pressure is therefore exerted. However, if the wind blows from the side or at an angle from forward the sail does not break the wind. Instead the wind is diverted by the sail's aerodynamic shape. The airflow is slowed on the nearer side and pressure increases. On the outer side airflow is accelerated and this results in a reduction in pressure which

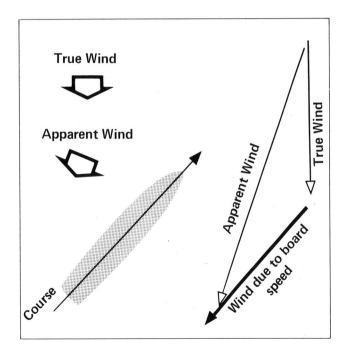

True Wind

Apparent Wind

Course

Apparent Wind

True Wind

Wind due to board speed

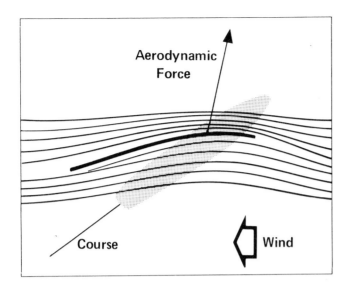

causes suction. Both forces combine to move the sailboard forward. The principle is the same as that of flight except that, in this case, the resultant force is not upwards as in the case of an aeroplane, but forwards or, to be more precise, not directly forwards but at an angle which is roughly at right angles to the surface of the sail. The reason why the sailboard does not also move in the same direction at right angles but instead sails straight ahead is its underwater body. The long immersed surface of the sailboard and the broad deep daggerboard resist sideways pressure and convert it into forward movement.

The Simulator

That is enough theory for now — it is time for you to take some practical steps. In sailboarding schools the instructor often gives you your first hours of practice on a simulator. This apparatus is exactly like a sailboard with sail, wishbone boom and all the component parts, but it is set up on land and is mounted on a turntable which has springs. The great advantage of the simulator is that the instructor stands close by you all the time and can correct immediately any mistakes that you make. Also, when you lose your balance, you do not land in the water but just jump down. This saves your energy and is far more encouraging than wearisome attempts which continually land you in the water.

A simulator is an ideal aid when learning. It comes close to giving you the feel of the conditions that prevail on the water and is used mainly to teach you the sequence of movements that you will use when sailboarding. The first practice session on the simulator is by far the most important. None of the problems that arise then, and to which you find the solution, should recur when you are on the water. The instructor will quietly make you aware of the principles of forward movement and you can then convert these principles into actual forward motion when you are out on the water.

On the pages which follow we have described the way to practise and alter course in such a way that you can either use the simulator or the sailboard itself.

The instructor can correct faults immediately when a simulator is used, and if you fall you do not land in the water.

Balance

The Way to Learn

- When practising how to balance leave the rig on land.
- Take the sailboard into thigh deep water and put the daggerboard in the slot.
- If the wind is blowing from the land remember that it will blow you and your board further offshore. Either tie yourself to an object on shore with a line made fast to the daggerboard beneath the board or get a friend to prevent the board drifting out to sea.
- Get on the board and try to balance on it with as relaxed a stance as possible. Do not contract the muscles of your legs and try to keep your knees, hips and ankles loose.
- Rock the sailboard about a little and then try to damp the movement.
- Stand on the daggerboard slot and turn yourself right round in a complete circle in both directions. You should not take the rig to the surfboard until you can do this easily.

The Position of Your Feet

Before you climb onto the sailboard with the rig, be sure that you know which end of the board is forward and which is aft. It often happens that, in the heat of the moment, learners become confused and try to sail backwards which, of course, results in an unintentional swim. The forward end, the bow, is where the board curves to a point. The after end, the stern, is easy to recognize because the daggerboard slot is aft of the mast. Be sure, too, that you know which part of the sail will be the forward edge. The forward side is where the wishbone boom is attached to the mast, while on the aft corner the sail is attached to the boom by the outhaul.

The time has now come to learn two more sailing terms, namely windward and leeward. Windward is the side that faces and is nearer to the wind. Leeward is the side that is further from the wind.
It is very important to check again the direction from which the wind is blowing and to make a mental note of this before you climb onto the board. Now turn your board so that it is lying at right angles across the wind and make sure that the mast is lying exactly in the direction in which the wind is blowing. The mast will therefore lie to leeward and you will climb aboard the sailboard from windward. Stand so that you have your back to the wind.
IMPORTANT: Generally speaking you must always stand on the board with your back to the wind.
The mast is lying directly in front of you at right angles to the sailboard. At this point be especially careful about the position of your feet. Both must be on the centreline, which is the imaginary fore-and-aft line between the bow and the stern. Your forward foot should be quite close to the mast and ahead of it, touching the mast foot, while your aft foot should be on the middle of the daggerboard slot. Note the

Before setting off, connect the uphaul to the foot with shock cord so that it is always ready to catch hold of near your feet.

position of your feet carefully because they must be back in the same positions after every exercise that you will carry out later.

The Starting Position (Mast Abeam)

At last it is time to start: the mast foot has been inserted in the step, you have climbed on the board with your back to the wind and the sail is lying to leeward. You now have to pull the rig out of the water. This is very easy on the simulator because the rig is not lying in the water but on the grass, and you

therefore only have to use as much strength as the weight of the rig requires. It is harder when you are afloat because water will have collected on the sail and in the mast sleeve, and this makes it quite heavy. You will need to use more strength when you are hoisting the rig until the water has run off the sail. There is a quite simple method however. Bend down and catch hold of the lower end of the uphaul with both hands but, before starting to pull, bend your knees slightly. As you raise the mast straighten your knees so that most of the load is taken by your thighs and not by your bent back. This will enable you to pull

This is the right way to get into the starting position. 1. The position of the feet: one leg just forward of the mast, the other on the daggerboard slot. 2. Always stand with your back to the wind. 3. Heave on the uphaul and bend your knees. 4. Straighten your legs when starting to pull up the rig, then move your hands along the uphaul from knot to knot. 5. Hold the rig by the uppermost knot and let it swing just clear of the water; this is the starting position.

up the first third of the rig without difficulty. The rest is easy enough using your arm muscles alone because most of the water will already have run off the sail. Pull the rig up gradually, working knot by knot along the uphaul and raising the mast until your hands are close under the boom. It is best to have a knot in the uphaul here so that you have a good grip. Your arms will be in front of you and slightly bent. Mast and boom will then be at right angles to the sailboard with the sail shaking in the wind while the wishbone boom will swing just over the surface of the water.

We will call this the starting position. Before getting under way always take up this position again.

Check now that everything is correct. You will be standing with your feet slightly apart, one foot just forward of the mast, the other on the daggerboard slot, your arms almost straight and your torso upright.

IMPORTANT: Slightly hollow your back and never stick your bottom out because you will always be off balance if your back is bent. Hips, ankles and knees should be relaxed to help you keep your balance. When you are in the mast abeam position the sail blowing to leeward tells you exactly the direction in which the wind is blowing. Later, if you get into difficulties, always revert to this starting position.

Chris Forstmeier shows here that sailboarding does not have to be a sport for strong men only. Ladies, too, can raise the rig without difficulty.

  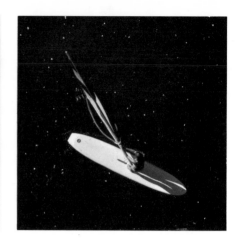

Practising Turning the Board

Beginning from this starting position, and still holding the uphaul with both hands, incline the mast aft towards the stern of the sailboard. At the same time transfer your weight to the aft foot. You will find that the board starts to turn round under the sail. As soon as the bow of the board comes close to the wind direction move slowly and carefully forward of the mast and round to the other side, still holding the uphaul with the sail shaking in the wind. Then press with your feet to turn the sailboard further, taking small steps, and continue turning the sailboard until you are back in your original position. You will have turned the sailboard through 360° beneath your feet. Try this several times, turning in both directions until you can do it easily; the harder the mast and sail are inclined against the pressure of the wind, the faster the board will turn.

Handling Techniques

Getting Under Way

Now at last the time has come to start sailing. We will change from the starting position to the sailing position. We use this term to describe the position of the body and the sails when the sailboard is moving straight ahead. First, however, there are two important terms to be defined — mast hand and sail hand.

- The mast hand is always forward on the boom near the mast, and it controls the angle of inclination of the mast.
- The sail hand is always aft on the boom, and is responsible for the position of the sail in relation to the wind.

The Way to Learn

Start from the mast abeam position in which your aft hand is holding the upper end of the uphaul, and then proceed as follows:

- First your front hand reaches over the aft hand (which continues to hold the uphaul) and grasps the wishbone boom immediately aft of the mast.
- Simultaneously release the uphaul and bring the rig across the board, so that the mast is inclined about 15 degrees to windward. You will need to twist your body to face the front of the board.
- Now grab the boom with your aft hand about a shoulder's width from your mast hand.
- Gently harden the sail with your aft hand. Harden means to pull the sail towards you against the pressure of the wind; ease out means to let the sail move away from you, easing the wind pressure.

You are now in the sailing position. The mast is inclined slightly to windward and the wishbone boom is approximately parallel to the surface of the water, your back is straight, your knees are slightly bent and relaxed, your forward arm is bent with your mast hand near the shoulder, your aft arm is not quite straight but slightly bent. Once you are in this position the board will gather way very quickly and you must

therefore carry out all these movements smoothly and without jerking so that you do not lose your balance.

Suggestions

- When in the sailing position always keep your back straight and slightly hollowed, with your bottom tucked in. Letting your torso bend forward is the worst mistake.
- Make sure you pull the rig far enough across the board with your front hand. In your normal stance you should only be able to see the front of the board through the windows. Two further suggestions will ensure that you adopt the correct position: (1) you should twist your torso so that your shoulders face the front of the board; (2) the mast should gently rest against the calf of your leading leg.
- When hardening the sail with your sail hand make sure you do not move the mast.
- If the wind is too strong ease the sail hand slightly.

Practise this sequence of movements for getting under way from the starting position again and again because they must be repeated every time you start off. Practise from both sides of the sailboard so that you do not find one side easier than the other. Always check your stance very carefully when in the sailing position. Successful sailboarding depends very largely on this.

Peter Brockhaus shows here how you can practise starting on the beach:
1. Support the rig by the uphaul

2. The mast hand passes over the uphaul and grasps the boom.

3. The mast hand supports the shaking sail.

4. The mast hand angles the sail past the torso

5. The sail hand catches hold of the boom.

6. Hardening the sail.

Altering Course

Now that you know how to keep a sailboard sailing straight ahead your next aim is to sail a curved course. First there are two more expressions to be learnt — luffing up and bearing away.

- Luffing up is to alter course to sail nearer to the wind, in other words, to sail a curve towards the wind.
- Bearing away is to alter course to sail further from the wind, or to sail a curve to leeward away from the wind.

As soon as you have learnt how to sail your sailboard in a straight line you should immediately try altering course. To be able to sail as straight as a die for a couple of hundred yards over the water is not enough, even if it is most satisfying in the excitement of the moment. What is far more important is to be able to steer your sailboard and to alter course so that you can return to the place from which you started.

There is a little more theory which must first be considered with regard to altering course. You will certainly have realized that the sailboard is quite different from a sailing boat in that it has no rudder, and yet it can be steered absolutely accurately. How does this happen?

The sail has an imaginary midpoint on which the whole force of the wind can be said to act, and this is called the centre of effort or CE. The power of the wind is transmitted to the sailboard through the mast foot, your hands, body and feet. The sailboard, for its part, has a centre of lateral resistance or CLR, and this point lies on the axis about which the board turns. If the CE lies directly over or slightly ahead of the CLR the board will sail straight ahead. This is what happens when the mast is inclined slightly to windward in the sailing position. If the mast is raked further forward the CE of the sail will also move

41

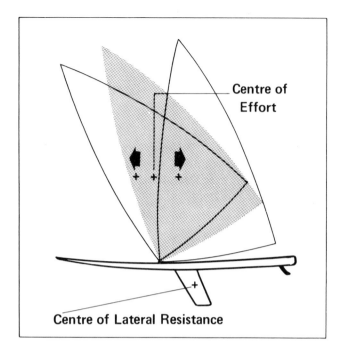

Centre of
Effort

Centre of Lateral Resistance

- In order to bear away from the sailing position, stretch the forward arm and bend the aft arm closer to your chest.
- In order to luff up rake the mast so far towards the stern that your aft arm is fully extended while your forward arm is bent close to your chest.

One arm is always fully extended while the other is fully bent.

Suggestion

When you have sailed a curve, the direction in which you are moving will have altered in relation to the direction of the wind and you will have to alter the position of the sail either by hardening it or easing it.

- *After bearing away you must ease out the sail.*
- *After luffing up you must harden the sail.*

And now some more sailing terms. The direction in which a surfboard sails in relation to the wind is called a point of sailing. When you are in the sailing position, steering a straight course with the wind abeam, the point of sailing is called a beam reach. If you luff up slightly you will be on a close reach and if you luff further you will be sailing close hauled. If you bear away you will at first be on a broad reach and if you continue to bear away you will run dead before the wind.

forward and the force of the wind consequently acts well forward of the CLR of the sailboard, pushing the bow away. This causes the sailboard to move in a curve away from the wind. You will bear away.

Exactly the opposite occurs when the mast is raked aft: the CE moves aft, the wind pushes the stern away and the sailboard curves up towards the wind. You luff up.

IMPORTANT: To bear away from the wind incline the mast further forward. To luff up towards the wind incline the mast aft.

A sailboard, therefore, is induced to luff up and bear away by raking the mast further aft or further forward along the centreline of the board. This is the completely new and extraordinarily simple method by which a sailboard steers.

42

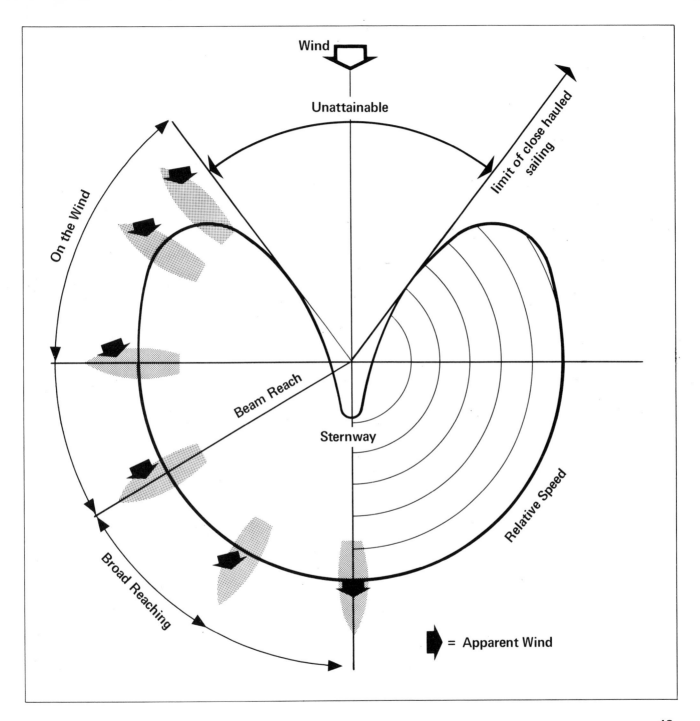

Wind

Unattainable

limit of close hauled sailing

On the Wind

Beam Reach

Sternway

Broad Reaching

Relative Speed

= Apparent Wind

Port and Starboard

You will certainly be familiar with the next two words to be defined, port and starboard, which are left and right in sailing language: use them because they are more precise than left and right.

- Starboard means the right hand side when looking towards the bow and the direction in which the board sails forwards.
- Port means the left hand side when looking towards the bow.

Similarly 'on port tack' means that the wind will be coming from the port side of the sailboard while the sail will be on the starboard side. When you are on starboard tack the wind will be blowing from starboard and the sail will be on the port or left hand side of the board.

You have already learnt how to sail on one tack on the different points of sailing from close hauled to running, hardening and easing the sail as you alter course. You will soon have noticed that the sailboard, like other sailing boats, reaches a limit: it cannot sail against the wind. The wind must be blowing at more than a certain angle to dead ahead, and this angle is approximately 45°. If you luff up so far that you are within this 45° zone you will find that the sail begins to shake, even when you have hardened it fully. The angle of attack is too small for the wind to be able to act on the surface of the sail and the result will be that you will first stop and then gradually drift backwards.

You now have two alternatives: you can either bear away and get sailing again on the same tack, or you can pass through this area of contrary wind and get on to the opposite tack by going about.

Going About or Tacking

Imagine that you are walking down a straight street and that the wind is blowing from your right. If you now walk back up the same street the wind will be blowing from your left. You have turned round and your opposite side faces the wind. If you wish to sail your surfboard back along the stretch of water you have just covered you must do the same and turn it so that the opposite side faces the wind. You go about onto the opposite tack.

You have already learnt the way in which you start going about; you luff up until you are almost head to wind. Now, however, the bows must pass right through the wind so that it blows onto the other side. Obviously you will not be able to stay on the same side of the board as before because you have to stand with your back to the wind.

The Way to Learn

- When sailing a straight course, in other words, when starting from the sailing position, luff up by inclining the mast aft. The sailboard begins to turn towards the wind.
- While turning, let go of the wishbone boom with your sail hand and catch hold of the uphaul. At the same time start to move round forward of the mast taking small steps. The mast hand lets go of the boom and also grasps the uphaul. Both hands will be by the uppermost knot immediately below the wishbone boom.
- You stand in exactly the same way as when you are in the starting position with arms only slightly bent and back straight.
- Now let the sail swing over the stern of the surfboard to the other side by letting the mast tilt away from you slightly, just as you did when practising turning the sailboard, and move carefully to the other side of the board taking small steps.

- You will have finished tacking when you are back in the starting position on the new side.
- Mast and sail will be at right angles to the board.
- The board will have turned through 180° and the bow will be pointing back in the direction from which you came.
- You now change from the starting position to the sailing position so as to get under way again.
- Practise this several times until you can go about perfectly, and practise starting from both port tack and starboard tack so that you do not develop a preference for one or the other.

When sailboarding the ability to tack well is extremely important.

Suggestions

- First practise going about quite slowly so that you can keep your balance while you are stepping round forward of the mast. It does not matter if your sailboard stops entirely or even drifts backwards.
- Until you have mastered the sequence of movements thoroughly do not try to luff rather faster while close hauling the sail. When you do this you get so much swing that the sailboard will turn through the eye of the wind of its own accord. You then only have to hold the uphaul briefly and step bravely round to the other side of the mast.

Back again to our straight course; you can now sail back and forth on alternate tacks with the wind abeam. There are two ways of changing to the opposite tack. You can either change with the wind blowing from forward or with the wind coming over the stern. The first method is going about or tacking, with the bow turning through the eye of the wind. The alternative, when the stern turns through the wind, is called gybing.

Gybing

Gybing a sailing boat is rather difficult and can be dangerous, especially in strong winds. It is quite different and much easier with a sailboard because the boom can be swung round over the bow on to the other side with a smooth series of movements.

The Way to Learn

- From sailing a straight course in the sailing position, bear away by inclining the mast forward. As the board bears away your sail hand catches hold of the uphaul. Then grasp the uphaul with your mast hand as well. The mast, tilting forward swings the sail over the bow. Both your feet must be placed aft of the mast while you do this, and you will face towards the bow. Back straight — arms almost fully stretched.
- Swing the sail around onto the other side until you are back in the starting position.
- Practise gybing several times until you are sure of the sequence of actions and have no more difficulty with keeping your balance. See pages 111–112 for further remarks on gybing.

On pages 46/47 Chris Forstmeier demonstrates the textbook method of going about. Here Peter Brockhaus shows how to gybe.

49

Gybing, when the sail is passed over the bow to the other side, this time viewed from above.

Running

This point of sailing, when you are moving in the same direction as the wind is blowing, will at first probably present the most difficulty due to the fact that it is not easy to keep your balance. You are no longer standing near the mast with your feet on the middle line but aft of the mast with your feet to port and starboard near the daggerboard slot, and this stance is by no means as stable as the sailing position. An added difficulty is that waves generally roll up under the sailboard from aft and cause it to see-saw awkwardly.

The Way to Learn

- From the sailing position take the mast forward and bear away.
- At the same time your forward foot, which is forward of the mast, is shifted further aft near the daggerboard slot. The other foot is placed on the opposite side of the daggerboard slot and preferably slightly further aft so that one foot is rather ahead of the other.
- You are now standing aft of the mast and are looking forward.
- When you have borne away so far that you are running dead before the wind, pull the sail in front of you so that it is at right angles to the wind and the direction in which you are sailing. The sail hand eases the sail out fully, while the mast hand rakes the mast sideways towards the side of the mast hand and beyond the edge of the board (in the direction which was windward).
- The sail now sets ahead of you in such a way that you can only see forward through the window — so keep a good lookout on the water ahead.

Beating to Windward

You know already that only one thing is impossible when sailboarding, and that is to sail against the wind. It is nevertheless possible to work up towards the direction from which the wind is blowing by means of beating on alternate tacks. *Beating is to sail a zig-zag course to windward.* This is slower than sailing with the wind abeam.

Two points are especially important when beating. You must always sail close to the wind, and you must be able to go about perfectly. These are the two factors involved when beating. First you sail close hauled, at an acute angle to the wind, then you go about and sail close hauled again on the other tack. Each time you go about you will have gained ground to windward and will gradually work up against the wind.

IMPORTANT: When beating you must always sail close to the wind and harden the sail as much as possible.

Practise beating assiduously because when there is an offshore wind, in particular, you will always be driven further out to seaward and you will need to be able to beat home to the shore.

Suggestions

- Go about quickly when beating. Then you will not be driven so far to leeward by the wind.
- Luff up quickly after going about so that you lose as little ground to windward as possible.
- Luff up as close to the wind as you can until you are just at the border line of the 45° area where the sail begins to shake. The sailboard will sail slower on this point of sailing than when the wind is abeam.
- It is often better to place the forward foot just aft of the mast foot when close hauled. This moves your weight further aft and the sailboard will not bore so readily into the waves which will be coming from ahead.
- If you have a board with a retracting daggerboard, make sure that it is properly down.
- Do not hold the boom so far in that the aft end is over the stern of the board. It will reduce speed to the point where you will eventually stop.

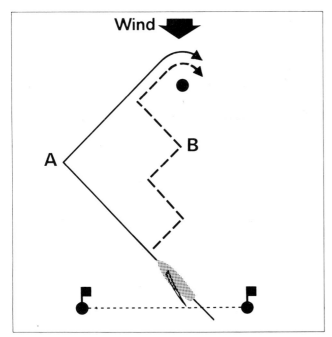

An objective that lies directly to windward can either be reached by making two long tacks (A) or by beating, using short tacks (B).

Turning Circles

And now, finally, the last practical exercise needed for passing a simple board sailing test. This exercise enables you to prove how well you have mastered the different points of sailing. It involves sailing a full circle.

- From the sailing position luff up until you are close hauled.
- Then go about quickly and smoothly without coming to a dead stop.
- Bear away gradually until you are running.
- Now gybe and return to the sailing position.

If you have carried out all the actions fluently and continuously you will be back at the place from which you started because you will have sailed round in a circle. You will also have proved to yourself that you can sail your sailboard to any desired point because this small circle that you have practised can be extended in any direction.

Turning a circle like this involves all that you first need to know when sailboarding because it includes going about, gybing and steering on the different points of sailing.

Suggestions

- First practise turning circles with a diameter of about 20 yards.
- When you can do this well try to sail to specific objectives such as buoys, piers or landmarks until you are quite certain that you can sail your sailboard to any point on the water.

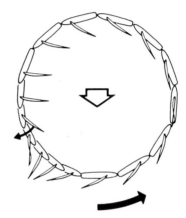

When you sail a full circle you learn how to go about and to gybe, and also how the sail should be set on all the different points of sailing.

Ken and Gordon Way compare Dufour and Trapezium booms on the Sea Panther when beating to windward. *Photo David Eberlin.*

Further Information That You Will Require

Right of Way Rules

You are not alone on the water when you are sailing. Generally you have to share the lakes, reservoirs or the coast with many others, including sailing boats, motor boats, naval vessels and, of course, swimmers. There are specific rules in force on all waters designed to prevent collisions, just as there are rules for traffic on the roads.

You must observe these rules carefully — for your own safety too — because yours is a very fast craft and any collision can cause severe damage and, what is worse, injure people. To date, no really serious accident has occurred when sailboarding. Please ensure that this state of affairs continues. In particular observe the following rules very carefully:

- Every sailboarder must behave on the water in such a way that no other vessel or person is endangered, damaged or injured, or unnecessarily impeded.

- Never sailboard where there are swimmers. Be especially careful because swimmers are often inquisitive and come to have a look at you, and it is often difficult to spot one head in the water, especially when there are waves. Just imagine what could happen if you sailed straight over a swimmer. He would probably be severely injured and you would be held responsible. Please, therefore, give all swimmers a wide berth.
- With this in mind always keep at least 100 yards from the bank or shore.
- Sailboards must give way to commercial and naval shipping.
- Do not sailboard in port entrances or near naval installations.
- Sailboards must keep clear of all vessels which are propelled by muscle power, such as rowing boats and canoes.
- In addition sailboards must abide by the internationally agreed rules which define right of way between sailing vessels.

1. A sailing boat or a sailboard which is on port tack must give way to a boat or sailboard sailing on starboard tack. Remind yourself by strapping red tape on the port side of the wishbone boom. Red means that you must give way, while green tape on the starboard half of the boom means that you have right of way.
2. If two boats or sailboards are sailing on the same tack the one to windward has to give way — leeward has right of way over windward.
3. Overtaking boats or sailboards must not hinder a vessel that is being overtaken.
- Sailboards must take avoiding action in good time, and in such a way that they can be seen to be taking decisive steps to avoid a collision.
- You are not allowed to enforce your right of way. If a boat or board that should give way to you does not do so you must avoid colliding with him. You may, however, call out to him to draw his attention to the fact that you have right of way.
- Sail your sailboard confidently and do not be afraid of other sailing boats. Generally speaking sailors know and abide by the rules of the road. In any case you are able to take avoiding action more quickly and easily than a 60 ft yacht, for example.
- If you should find yourself in a really ticklish situation at some time it is best simply to let the sail drop into the water and you will then stop immediately.
- A stop gybe is a rather more elegant alternative. You simply swing the sail quickly over the bow to the other side. The sailboard will turn 180° and, from full speed ahead, come to an immediate stop.

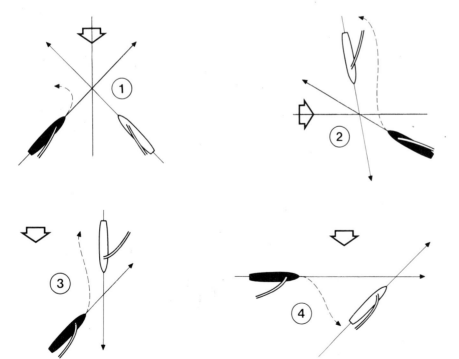

Opposite tacks: Figures 1, 2 and 3 show which board has right of way when they are on opposite tacks. In each case the black board on port tack has to give way. It is rather more complicated when the boards are on the same tack.
Same tack: Figure 4. The sailboard that is pointing higher has right of way. The windward board gives way to the board to leeward.

The Weather

Sailboarding is a sport dependent on wind and weather, and the weather is often ill-tempered and sometimes downright capricious. There are two limits to sailboarding — flat calms and storms.

The flat calm is the lesser evil, for then the sailboard just stops on the water and cannot be steered. There is a way of reaching the nearest shore in spite of a flat calm. You just convert your sailboard into a paddling board. Drop the sail on the water, take the mast foot out of the step and fold the rig up as you do on land. The sail can either be removed or rolled around the mast. There are several ways of paddling. — You can lay all the parts lengthwise on the sailboard with nothing trailing in the water, kneel on them, and paddle with your hands.

- You can pull out the daggerboard and kneel or sit on the sailboard using the daggerboard as a paddle.
- You can sit or kneel on the sailboard and paddle with the mast. In this case you must of course remove the sail and fold it up. It has been found from experience that this is the simplest and fastest method of making way without wind.

Strong winds often give the sailboarding beginner a lot of trouble, so be careful to check on the weather conditions before you go out on the water. Listen to the weather forecast on the radio and ask local sailors about any peculiarities in the weather in their area.

Basically you should never go out on the water when a thunderstorm is brewing nearby because the lightning and the strong gusts which strike suddenly make thunderstorms the greatest danger to threaten us on the water.

Sailboarding in strong winds or stormy weather calls for great skill, and is fully covered in the second part

of this book. It may happen, however, that you as a beginner are unintentionally caught out by a storm and do not see any possibility of returning to the shore under sail. You have several alternatives.

- De-rig the sailboard and paddle to the nearest shore, just as in a flat calm. You should not attempt to paddle against the wind because you will make little or no forward progress in spite of using all your strength.
- Stand in the starting position with the mast at right angles to the sailboard and your back to the wind, but let the end of the boom and some of the sail drag in the water. The wind will then only be able to act on part of the sail but will nevertheless drive you forward relatively quickly. You can only use this method when the wind is blowing parallel to the shore as you will then be able to reach the land with the wind abeam.
- If the wind is blowing hard onshore, put both feet aft of the mast and face forward with the sail shaking over the bow. Your back will present a sufficiently large area to the wind which will blow you forward, sometimes quite fast.

If there is a strong offshore wind it may well be that it is impossible to paddle back to the shore. In this case it is best to let the sail fall into the water where it will act as a sea anchor. Should you find yourself in difficulty and see no possible way of getting back to land by your own efforts you can use the following internationally recognized distress signals:

- Shout loudly or whistle.
- Wave both hands over your head (but never do this just when waving to your friends because unnecessary rescue attempts could immediately be set in train).

If you find yourself in such a situation always stay with your sailboard, even if you think that you can swim to the shore. You can ride out any storm on the sailboard.

56

IMPORTANT: If you set off in uncertain weather, please tell your friends or acquaintances on land so that they notice that you are missing in case of emergency and can initiate rescue operations.

Another point: storm warnings are given on some inland European waters and along some coasts. Flashing lights or a red signal on the shore may be seen or sirens heard. If you are on the water when such storm warnings are given you must return immediately to the nearest part of the shore.

Once you have mastered all that is covered in this beginners' section of the book you should try to answer the following questionnaire which covers approximately those requirements that figure in the basic theory test. Should you find any question difficult, please turn back and read the appropriate pages of the book again. Questions 1, 3 and 15 are covered in the second part of this book.

The Express board with Trapezium boom. *Photo Tim Masters.*

Test Questions

Practical Test

1. Rigging a sailboard correctly.
2. Starting and sailing a straight course.
3. Stopping with the wind abeam (emergency stop).
4. Tacking and gybing without coming to a halt.
5. Bearing away from a beam reach to a dead run.

The practical test should be carried out in winds of force 3 or less and in normal seas.
It is preferable to use a buoy to mark out a course. The applicant should have completed a 5-7 hour course in an authorized sailboarding school. Only in exceptional cases can the test be taken without having completed such a course.

Theory Questions

1. What clothing should a sailboarder wear?
2. What are the internationally recognized distress signals for sailboards afloat?
3. What alterations are made to the sailboard in strong offshore winds with a view to safety?
4. What are the three most important rules of the road for sailing vessels, and therefore also for sailboarders?
5. What waters should you avoid when sailboarding?
6. Sailboarders should be especially careful of certain people involved in water sports. Which?
7. Of what should the sailboarder practising on the water take especial care?
8. How are storm warnings given, and what action should be taken?
9. The inhaul is tied with which knot in order to attach the boom to the mast?
10. What is important when transporting a sailboard on the roof of a car?

11. Of what must the sailboarder beware when in shallow water?
12. How do you keep a look out on the water ahead when your sailboard is on a run?
13. How do sailboarders generally start to go about?
14. Define the expressions windward and leeward.
15. How do you alter the shape of the sail for strong winds and light breezes?
16. How do you stop your sailboard when you are moving at full speed?

Part 2

Advanced Techniques

Sailboarding in Winds of over Force 4
Beaufort Scale

With your first experiences of sailboarding behind you, you will have found that you have learnt this new sport much more quickly than you would have believed possible during your first hours on the sailboard. Now, when you climb onto the board, your knees no longer tremble and even raising the rig presents no problem. You may perhaps already have tried to sail a longer distance out to sea and back again. Gradually you become confident in winds of increasing strength.

When a gust strikes you lean out backwards, harden the sail, and off you go. You no longer sail with your weight concentrated above the sailboard, but you push the board sideways away from you and hang out near the board, close above the water. The first time that the spray really flew you probably came back with a proud grin on your face because you had got wet without falling in. You seemed to fly over the water astonishingly fast — and yet that was only a foretaste of what you can experience with your sailboard.

Just be more confident! Then, with the help of the following chapters on sailboarding technique, and with determination, you will be able to reach a standard of performance which will mark you as a real sailboarder.

Make no mistake about one fact, however. When the wind is blowing at over force 4 everything seems to be entirely different. If you do not know how to gauge the strength of the wind without an anemometer, look carefully at the table in the appendix. You can estimate the wind strength by observing the state of the surface of the water. You will also realize that there is another easy way of recognizing the critical borderline between force 4 and force 5 — you will suddenly find that you are falling into the water far more frequently than hitherto. It is enough to drive you to despair! Everything which you thought you had learnt seems to have been blown away. It just does not work. You are at the force 4 performance plateau and everybody suffers when they reach this stage. The same occurs in many other sports and, in order to surmount this hurdle, you have to start at the beginning again to a certain extent.

Suppose we take skiing as an example. You have learnt how to do graceful swings down a well pisted slope, and everything goes smoothly and easily. But suddenly, in deep snow or on a steeper piste covered with moguls, you cannot swing any more. You tighten up and become unsure, losing the rhythm of the correct movements. The only cure is to keep calm, study your mistakes, and go back to practising in easier conditions.

When you find yourself in this uncertain state on your sailboard for the first time, do not fight on despairingly because this will be no help. It is far better to learn to understand thoroughly how your sailboard functions, and to find out more about its sailing characteristics before you attempt to sail in such winds. First read the following chapters carefully, and for your own safety assimilate the basic facts given so that you do not come to grief due to poor materials or an inadequately rigged sailboard.

Breathtakingly exciting: Sailboarding in a wind of over force 4. This is European champion Derk Thijs at Bendor.

The Board and its Parts

The information on sailboards which follows is based on the Windsurfer and the Windglider because these boards are the most widespread and have been longest in use. Obviously there are some aspects of sailboard construction which can be the subject of endless discussion. We will point out these controversial aspects and also comment on differences in the construction of other sailboards. It is important that you should learn to judge how well the individual parts of the sailboard function and also their load-bearing limits.

The Board

Even at a first glance the **shape** of the board reminds you of the surfboards which have been used for decades all around the world for wave-riding and surfing. The Windsurfer board is merely longer and broader because it not only has to support you but the rig as well. It must also be sufficiently buoyant to support you when you are standing motionless on it, rather than when you are riding a wave as is the case when you are surfing. Its origins explain why it performs at its best in waves or in breaking surf, and its qualities are not so apparent on smooth waters. Here a longer and less beamy sailboard such as the Windglider-Spider or the Surf Sailer Turbo is faster. The normal sailboard, however, is a very good compromise for use both in smooth water and in high breakers because heavy breaking surf calls for a shorter board. What is required then is that the sailboard should move well with the seas, and not extend so far over them that it slams hard and suddenly.

The amount of sheer is an important factor when considering the shape of the surfboard because the bow of a surfboard must curve up forward sufficiently. If it does not curve up enough the surfboard will tend to cut under the waves and will also be slow to start planing on the surface of the water. You can check whether there is enough sheer by laying the board on a level surface and weighting the stern down until it touches the surface. The tip (bow) should curve up about 7½-8 inches above the stern. Do not keep your board where it is very hot, or in other trying conditions. It is best to store it standing up against a wall, lying on one side, or suspended by means of loops of rope or webbing hung from the ceiling of a garage or shed.

One of the most controversial points debated by sailboard sailors is the question of the material of which the sailboard is constructed. There are some who swear by fibreglass and will not consider anything else, while others prefer polyethylene or similar softer plastics. If you wish to consider objectively the advantages and disadvantages of both materials, study the summary which follows. It lists the most important qualities required for a sailboard, and shows how fibreglass and polyethylene compare.

These polyethylene boards have the classically beautiful shape of surfing boards.

	Fibreglass	Polyethylene
Toughness	−	+
Impact resistance	−	+
Finish	+	+
Ease of repair	+	−
Resistance to heat	+	−
Resistance to ultra violet rays	+	−
Adhesion of skin and foam	−	+
Roughening of the standing surface	−	+
Accuracy of moulding	+	+
Joints between the parts	−	+
Specific weight	1.27	0.92

Blowmoulding overcomes most of the drawbacks of polyethylene.

You must decide for yourself which characteristics are the most important to you. One man will prefer a perfect finish while another considers a good foothold on the sailboard more important. A supporter of fibreglass is pleased to be able to make repairs easily, while the advocate of polyethylene enjoys the fact that no major damage results if he lets his sailboard fall on a stone.

One problem is common to all boards. In order to keep the weight low the outer skin has to be very thin and, in time, small dents will occur. These must not be confused with blisters. Dents are relatively harmless and show that the skin adheres well to the foam inside. Blisters, on the other hand, where the skin has worked free are very unpleasant as the extremely vulnerable foam inside will gradually rub away. Take your sailboard to an expert if blisters start to appear, and do not wait until the board has become soft. He may possibly be able to repair the damage by adding foam or by renewing the adhesive.

You will know as a result of your first hours of sailboarding how important it is to have a good, non-slip surface to stand on. Above all avoid sliding about on the sailboard with an oiled body. If the board becomes covered with anti-sunburn oil only a thorough cleaning with an alcohol-based fluid will remove it properly. There is a quite finely roughened surface on the Windsurfer, and this gives a good foothold, especially to bare feet, and also to gym shoes. It is particularly good because it does not graze the skin. Test the surface on which you stand when it is wet and remember that, in water, your skin becomes more vulnerable than usual to sharp edges and rough surfaces. This point is of course relevant in respect of all the parts of your sailboard, and a good board must be kindly to swimmers all round the sides.

The Daggerboard

The importance of the daggerboard has been underestimated by surfers until now. At times one can only be surprised at the discussions which take place on shore. Every minor crease in the sail is criticized, the smallest unevenness on the sailboard is found fault with, and the underwater surface of the sailboard is even rubbed down to increase speed. At the same time the man with whom we are discussing the sailboard may well be using a daggerboard which is unworthy of its name. It may be just a simple piece of board, strong and perhaps slightly rounded along the leading and trailing edges, but often it has not been streamlined at all.

You may ask why sailboards are equipped with such basic daggerboards, and the makers' reply is that they make daggerboards like this intentionally because a daggerboard must be tough to stand up to misuse by beginners who frequently run aground. They add that if anyone wants to improve his daggerboard he can rub it down himself to give it a good streamlined cross section. This argument cannot be dismissed out of hand because the normal daggerboard is certainly adequate for general work, and naturally is also stronger than the fast daggerboards we are about to describe.

The ideal cross section for a daggerboard is known both from hydrodynamic theory and from boat building experience. From the rounded leading edge, it should progress smoothly to a maximum thickness a third to a half way back from the leading edge, and then gradually fair off to a sharp edge aft. This allows water to stream past smoothly while eddies, which slow a sailboard, will only appear at considerably higher speeds than when a normal daggerboard is used. In addition to this a properly streamlined daggerboard defers for a considerable time the moment at which the problem of daggerboard planing starts. This phenomenon occurs when the sailboard is travelling at high speed and suddenly becomes unstable, the result being a capsize fall (see p. 118).

Wood is the ideal material if a daggerboard is to be streamlined easily by a handyman without the need for complicated tools. Nevertheless it should not just be any old wood but good marine plywood or mahogany. If it is made of mahogany check too that it is not made of solid wood, but of three laminations glued together with the grain of the central piece running across that of the two outer layers. This will prevent the daggerboard warping in sun and water. Although the one design philosophy of the IWCA is strict many alterations to racing daggerboards are permitted. They can be shaped as desired, made shorter and narrower, or rubbed down and all manner of finishes applied. However, increasing the area is forbidden, whether by adding on extra pieces or, as is also possible, by sinking the daggerboard lower in the case. This is simple enough in principle; the wooden battens at the top of the daggerboard which prevent it slipping through the slot need only to be removed and replaced with hard rubber. The daggerboard can then be pushed deeper into the slot with the result that the area beneath the surfboard is increased. The advantage this gives over other competitors would be detected immediately in a race because the sailboard is able to sail closer to the wind. Another advantage would be gained if the

Normal daggerboard

Shaped racing daggerboard

Charculla storm daggerboard

Hawaii surf daggerboard

daggerboard were brought further aft, making the sailboard less eager to luff up to windward, and also making it easier to sail in heavy weather.

If you have a racing daggerboard which is perfectly shaped and are proud of its smoothly finished surface, never use it in shallow water or on surfing beaches where you can easily run aground. Keep this daggerboard purely for racing and use a less precious daggerboard for everyday sailboarding. Any sailboarder who practises his sport intensively, who wants to get the best from his sailboard and who puts everything into sailboarding, should undoubtedly possess several daggerboards. We are thinking primarily about the special heavy weather daggerboards and those for use in breaking surf which we will now describe.

The simplest way to make a heavy weather dagger-board is to take a normal racing board and to saw off about 4¾ inches forward and 6 to 7¾ inches from the lower edge. The leading edge must then be rounded off well and the board shaped with a rasp and emery paper. Such a daggerboard has two advantages:

- It draws less and can therefore be used closer to the beach.
- The reduced surface area of the daggerboard makes reaching and running easier and defers the danger of capsize falling until really high speeds are reached.

These advantages are common to all heavy weather daggerboards, but they also have their disadvantages and these should not be overlooked.

- The area of the daggerboard is considerably reduced and it is therefore impossible to sail so close to the wind.
- There is no improvement over the normal racing daggerboard when hitting the bottom because the board does not angle up through the daggerboard slot, and the case can be damaged.

This heavy weather daggerboard can therefore only be recommended if you wish to avoid spending money on another design and instead prefer to make your own heavy weather board from one that is to hand.

An original alternative is the Charculla storm dagger-board developed by the surfing enthusiasts, the

Charculla brothers. From the start the twins were more interested in heavy weather sailing than in racing, and they therefore concentrated on seeing how they could best adapt their sailboard. As the photograph shows, the surface area of the dagger-board is the same as that of a normal racing board but is concentrated further aft. This daggerboard therefore both retains the full surface area to prevent sideways motion (leeway) and also moves the centre of lateral resistance (CLR) of the sailboard further aft. This means that the mast can be taken further aft in strong winds without the sailboard luffing up due to the fact that the centre of effort of the sails and the CLR are still above one another. The Charculla storm daggerboard is not without its disadvantages however.

- Because of its shape it has to be shipped from below the daggerboard case and therefore cannot be taken out while sailing. You are therefore denied the pleasure of sailboarding without a daggerboard (see p. 132).
- In its normal form it is not well enough stream-lined, or to be more precise, it is not shaped at all and this causes the eddies to appear which detract from performance at higher speeds.
- Due to its greater fore-and-aft length it increases directional stability at faster speeds in high seas. When using a Charculla storm daggerboard it is not possible to take so much advantage of the formation of the individual waves because the sail-board keeps sailing straight ahead. The consequence can be that the sailboard will bore be-neath a wave although it would have been easy enough to divert onto other waves a few yards away, using a more conventional daggerboard. This can also happen when surfing with a wave.

The surf-riding experts from Kailua Beach in Hawaii, on the other hand, have developed the Hawaii surf daggerboard specifically for use in breakers. They deliberately forego having a large lateral area because, on Kailua Beach, the waves that are mastered by Larry Stanley and his friends are so high that European surfers would not venture into them. A daggerboard for use in breaking surf, such as that shown in the photograph on page 69, should give as much directional stability as is required for getting under way from a standstill or after going about. The small lateral area (all that part of the sailboard which is underwater and offers resistance to leeway) is especially beneficial because it is then easier to drift with the waves, deliberately sliding sideways and making better use of their thrust. However the lateral area is inadequate when it comes to sailing close to the wind, or when making headway over a current, and this daggerboard can therefore only be recommended for experts who wish to sail in heavy breaking surf.

The Hawaii surf daggerboard has other advantages in that it can be removed from the surfboard while

Thilo Riedel's combination daggerboard in the down position as used for racing. . .

70

...and when used as a storm daggerboard with the centre of lateral resistance moved further aft.

under way and, when the ground is struck, it is pushed up through the daggerboard slot at an angle. This avoids damage to the case, which occurs all too easily with normal daggerboards in breaking surf.

The best daggerboard produced so far for use in both heavy weather and breaking surf is one developed by Thilo Riedel from Salzburg, and he calls it the combination daggerboard. It offers virtually all the advantages of the heavy weather and breaking surf daggerboards described above, but at the same time has almost the same lateral area as a normal racing daggerboard.

- As the photograph shows it can be used like a racing daggerboard and both the lateral area and the CLR almost coincide with those of the original Windsurfer daggerboard when it is in the down position.
- When used in the aft position draft is reduced and the CLR moves aft in the same way as with the Charculla daggerboard. Naturally a half way position can also be used.
- It can be worked with one foot and there is therefore little risk involved if, for example, you are

bearing away from close hauled and want to increase your speed. One step and the daggerboard is moved aft. Equally you only have to step on the protruding part to return the daggerboard to its original position.

- Damage to the daggerboard slot is avoided, even when running aground violently, because the shock of the impact is well distributed.
- Finally, it can be pulled out of the daggerboard slot from above when no longer required, or when it is a hindrance — for example when entering breaking surf.

If your daggerboard is supplied with a cord attached you can make a simple and effective improvement by replacing the cord with a strip of broad woven tape with which you can pull the board out. Cord can be very unpleasant when you are surfing with the daggerboard removed and have it hanging over your arm. It gets blown about and twisted round by the wind and by bumping against your body, with the result that the cord cuts badly into your arm. It is also much easier to pull the daggerboard out by a tape band when it sticks too firmly in the slot as is sometimes the case, perhaps due to sand. Remove the battens on the top of the board which prevent it slipping too far into the slot, and screw both ends of the woven tape under the batten. Do not screw the batten down too firmly onto the daggerboard. It should give if you run aground because it is easier to repair the batten than either the daggerboard itself or the daggerboard slot. A further suggestion to protect the slot from damage: use a saw to round off the forward part of the daggerboard where it sits in the slot so that it can slide up more easily if you hit the bottom. Filing down all the sharp corners until they are well rounded also helps to prevent damage to the slot.

While we are on this subject we should also warn you of the danger to your daggerboard slot if you run

aground with the daggerboard half raised. As we have already said, a well-streamlined daggerboard should taper to a fine edge aft. If this edge cuts into the slot it acts almost like a knife, and could well make a slit in the surfboard if it failed to break. So, be careful about running aground with a half raised daggerboard!

That should be enough on the subject of daggerboards. Which daggerboards, when, and how best to use them will follow in the sections on sailboarding in strong winds, breaking surf and waves.

The Fin

If you want to discover what effect the fin (or skeg) has on your sailboard just for once unscrew this small fitting which seems so unimportant and try boarding without it. You will then discover that your board simply will not sail straight and that each small wave calls for an alteration to the set of the sail. Later you will learn that you can sail easily without a daggerboard, but you will experience problems without a fin.

You would therefore be wise always to carry a spare fin in your sail bag, together with screws with which to attach it. Keep them safe by sticking them to the fin with tape. Then a boarding weekend or a holiday will never be spoilt because you have broken or lost your fin. Just as was the case with the daggerboard, keen boarders should not be content with the shape of the fin as supplied. Basically it should have the same streamlined cross section — in other words, thicker forward and tapering smoothly aft. A flat fin is not nearly so good as far as flow is concerned. In any case the streamlining of the fin is far less important than that of the daggerboard due to the fact that it is so much smaller.

A long drawn-out fin is not advisable for wave-riding and surfing in breakers, or for speedy tacking. It often gives the board too much directional stability and

The fin of
a Windsurfer

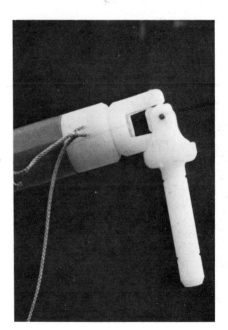

A Windglider's
mast foot

73

makes it difficult to luff up or bear away quickly. This is why many Windglider-Spider owners remove the fin entirely to make the sailboard easier to control. Wave-jumping boards, however, require increased directional stability and therefore usually have twin skegs.

The fin of some sailboards is identical to that of the surfboard as used in classic surfing. This shape has proved effective and certainly provides the best compromise between directional stability and ease of turning. There is a disadvantage, however, in that it can be dangerous. It is true that, up to now, no serious accident has occurred with these boards, but that is no reason for being careless. Never stand your sailboard against a wall or a fence with the bow pointing downwards, and therefore with the fin up high. The slightest breeze can throw the board over, and a passer-by could be injured by the fin. The fin could also be the cause of injury in breaking surf and when capsize falling, so take care.

The danger of breaking the fin is considerably less than is often assumed because those of most sailing surfboards are made of very strong nylon. However, anyone who surfs frequently in shallow waters can buy a safety fin which can neither cause injury nor break because it is made of rubber.

The HiFly's mast foot with adjustable release tension. When the required degree of tension has been pre-set by the internal cone, the foot is slipped into the socket and then locked in place by a half turn on the knurled ring. It will then only release at the required tension, but turning the locking ring again enables it to be taken out more easily.

The Mast Foot

The flexible joint at the foot of the mast is the part of the sailboard which has most influence on the sailing technique of sailboarding. Although it has been used for many years as a link in the transmission of mechanical power, a universal joint has never before been used in a sailing boat to enable the mast to be inclined in all directions and also turned lengthwise.

The ability of the rig to turn will not concern us further at this point. What interests us here are the two linkages which are also affected by the universal joint: the connection with the board and the connection with the mast.

There is virtually no part of the Windsurfer that has caused surfers more annoyance than the famous, or infamous T-piece, the piece of wood which connects the lower end of the universal joint to the sailboard. This annoyance is partly justified because, originally, the T-piece was not sufficiently well made, but it is also mainly unjustified because the correct function of the mast-to-sailboard connection was not recognized.

We shall start with the most important point, the way in which the mast foot anchorage functions. Its purpose can be stated clearly. The mast foot must be anchored so firmly in the mast step in the sailboard that it does not come out when the rig is raised, but it must also be free enough to come out of its own accord in certain circumstances. It can be said to have the same purpose as the safety bindings on skis: in normal skiing they must give proper control of the skis, but in dangerous moments the safety bindings must release.

What, then, are the dangerous moments when sail-boarding? Firstly, all those occasions when, in strong winds or with a slippery board, one foot slips down to the leeward side of the mast while the sailboarder falls and sits on the windward side of the board. When the mast is blown down to leeward by the wind his leg could be crushed and severely injured if the foot of the mast did not not come out of the mast step. Such accidents have occurred already, so this dangerous moment is not just theory.

The second dangerous situation relates to the sail-board itself. The danger of breaking the mast and the boom is considerably increased if the mast foot cannot come out of the step. When you have once seen what can happen to a sailing surfboard which has been picked up by a breaker and thrown ashore you will understand immediately what is meant here. As soon as the top of the mast or the end of the boom touches the ground the mast foot must come out of the mast step immediately if nothing is to break. The fixed mechanical anchorage used by some sailboard manufacturers is therefore an unfortunate solution, and not a 'safety binding'.

Naturally, too slack a mast foot anchorage is also un-satisfactory, not so much because the mast foot slips out on every occasion and hits your legs, but rather because of the danger that, if you fall when a strong offshore wind is blowing, it is impossible to swim fast enough to catch the sailboard which is being blown along without the rig. Above force 5, therefore,

The drawing shows how a safety line is used to attach the mast foot to the daggerboard.

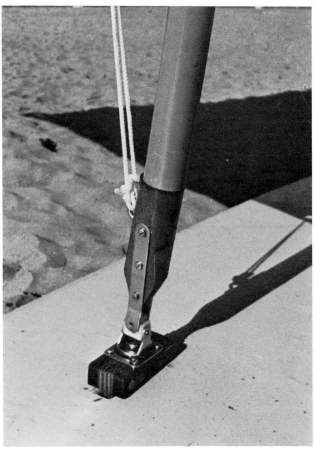

The Windsurfer's mast foot.

always rig a safety line which connects the dagger-board to the foot of the mast so that the board cannot drift away (see drawing).

You can very easily ensure that your Windsurfer has a good mast foot anchorage. First check the quality of the T-piece critically. Check whether it is one of those that was glued and nailed because you can not sail at all if your T-piece is broken and this type has been known to fail. If you are going to sail in heavy weather make a habit of being extremely careful to check this important part of the surfboard. It is certainly true that a sailboard has advantages as to safety over most sailing boats because there is no danger of capsizing, but this advantage is worthless if you are left drifting on the water with a broken T-piece.

The same can be said when it comes to the mast, boom and sail which also must be replaced or expertly repaired when necessary if they are to stand up to hard conditions when sailboarding.

The T-piece at the mast foot must be made of good mahogany and held together with two long screws. Both screws must be of stainless steel and countersunk.

To return to achieving correct mast foot anchorage. First check the gap between the T-piece and the mast step slot in the sailboard. Make sure that there is no sand in the step or on the foot because sand makes a bad joint. Now wrap several layers of 1¼ or 1½ in adhesive woven tape around the T-piece and check its seating in the mast step. Make a habit of not borrowing the mast foot of other sailing surfboards and thrusting them forcibly into your step. If you do this the foam inside the board will give in time. Nor should you pull wildly at the mast foot if it is sometimes difficult to remove due to sand. Many surfers have torn away the polyethylene skin from the foam in this way and ruined their sailboards. If the foam is soft already, send your board to be repaired immediately before the damage becomes worse. There is the same danger with fibreglass sailboards. Fibreglass is tougher, it is true, but does not adhere well to polyurethane foam.

A last piece of advice in connection with the mast foot: check occasionally that all the screws are driven well home. If they cannot be tightened because the threads have worn, replace the part or use longer screws.

The mast foot of the sailboard is attached to the sail by means of the luff downhaul, and the mast must therefore fit well over the foot. Woven adhesive tape can be used here too if there is excessive play between the wooden foot and the mast, but remember that wood always swells slightly when damp.

The mast must also be free to turn on the mast foot. There is a widespread bad habit among sailboarders of binding the mast foot and the mast together with tape or, as is also seen, of joining them together permanently with plastics.

Make your mast watertight by putting a cork or a polystyrene plug in the mast, and this must of course be pushed far enough in so that it does not prevent the mast foot sliding home. If the mast foot and mast cannot turn about each other at this point you run the risk of breakage. You will understand why if you take a well set up rig, with the inhaul connecting the boom closely to the mast as is correct. Lay your sailboard on the bank as normal, but be careful not to damage the fin. Insert the mast foot in the step of the sailboard with the sail lying flat on the ground. If you now take the end of the boom and raise it — in other words, if you move the mast longitudinally — you will see what strains are put on the universal joint if the mast and mast foot are fixed firmly together. Either the plastic part of the universal joint will break at some time, or the inhaul will part, and the step in the sailboard will be extremely overstressed. The mast foot must therefore be able to turn at least 90°.

In the case of the Windglider and other more modern boards, this caution is unnecessary as the mast foot mechanisms have been designed to avoid these problems.

Mast and Mast Top

The mast of the Windglider and Windsurfer is made of many thin layers of fibreglass mat laid around a tapered plug, and it is this that gives it its special durability and flexibility. Later you will be astonished at what it has to stand up to, and will then also realize why a sailboard's mast has to be such a first-rate product.

The Windsurfer mast top is of wood and should be smoothed off so that the top is slightly domed. This simple measure gives you two astonishing results. Firstly, the sail does not chafe through as it does when the end is cylindrical, even when the mast pocket is reinforced. Secondly the sail sets better up high because the unpleasant crease at the upper part of the leech will disappear. The junction between the

77

mast and the mast top must be made waterproof with adhesive tape so that no water can find its way into the mast. Again, the Windglider has been designed with an integral plastic mast top so that this problem does not occur.

Some sailboard manufacturers use alloy masts. These are generally double sleeved to achieve the required strength characteristics when compared with flexibility. Their advantages lie in relative cheapness and greater stiffness which prevents sail distortion in high winds. Their disadvantages lie primarily in excessive weight and the risk of getting bent in accidents.

Basically you should aim for a high quality mast. An inexpensive mast is certainly not the cheapest answer, because it will break too easily and probably give a poor sail shape in strong winds.

The Shark Surfer's boom. The sail is divided into two.

The Wishbone Boom

The wishbone boom, like the universal joint, is an essential feature of a sailboard, and as such its design holds implications for the performance of the craft. Though the original Windsurfer boom is made of mahogany, the majority of booms are now made from light aluminium alloy. Continuing development in this modern sport has naturally produced some very fine design features (see photos on p.79) which offer the following advantages:

- Aluminium booms weigh about half as much as those of mahogany, and allow the rig to be raised easily from the water.
- Rubber covering not only gives the board sailor a more comfortable and positive grip, but also offers a degree of insulation against the cold.
- A rubber handle at the inhaul end allows the rig to be held easily and comfortably when not sailing.
- Cleats for inhaul and overhaul lines not only make rigging far simpler but, by use of the outhaul line, offer the facility for adjusting the sail whilst sailing. Pulleys at the aft end of the boom help such adjustment.
- Finally, it must be remembered that the boom should be stiff, for if it bends (which often occurs in strong winds) the following problems may be noted:

- The boom interferes with the sail shape.
- The length of the boom is reduced and the tautly stretched sail becomes loose and, therefore, badly set. (This particular problem is one reason why some British boards use trapezium-shaped booms.)

To our way of thinking it is unnecessary to wrap bicycle tubes or tape around a mahogany wishbone boom provided you avoid getting anti-sunburn oil on your hands. If you have any difficulty in holding onto

The front boom fitting of the Dufour Wing has a handy notch for jamming the inhaul.

The Windglider's boom is now delivered with a rubber protective snubber.

the boom, make a resin paste like that used by sportsmen and athletes who have to grasp wooden objects. The disadvantage of wrapping something round the boom is that damp remains beneath it, and this shortens its life. We must remember, then, that a good wishbone boom must above all give a good handhold, and be so strong that it only bends a little.

For those readers who have a sailing surfboard with an alloy boom, we have another tip. The best material to wrap around the boom is the tape used for bicycle handlebars (cf. p. 24).

If you have experienced a catapult fall (see p. 122) at full speed, and the rig has suddenly been torn from your hands towards the bow, you will know why there has to be a snubber at the forward end of the boom. This will prevent a hole being made in your surfboard on such occasions, and you should not therefore buy a boom without a snubber unless you intend to make your own. Ideally it should be made of relatively soft and shock resistant material. Later, when the wind is very strong, you yourself may be hit hard by the rig, so the snubber is also required for your own protection. Be careful, though, if you are attaching a homemade snubber to an alloy boom and be sure not to cause the boom to leak. Every extra screw or rivet increases the danger of getting water inside the alloy tube.

There is another important point to consider in the case of the Windsurfer boom if it is to last for a long time. Make sure that the two ends of the boom are always tied together with a bowline. You will not then lose the outhaul and, what is more important, the ends of the boom cannot come apart and bend the W-shape fitting at the forward end.

A last piece of advice with regard to the boom: check that the screws or rivets on the fittings have not worked loose before you go out on the water in heavy weather. If the boom breaks under way it is just about impossible to make a temporary repair.

79

The Sail

Now we come finally to what is virtually the engine of the sailing surfboard — the sail itself. The most heated discussions take place between surfers (as they do between sailors) on this subject because when competitors are equally skilful it is the sail that is the decisive factor when it comes to winning races. The material, size and cut ought to be identical for all Windsurfers in order to comply with the one design philosophy, but unfortunately this has not been achieved.

The most important characteristics required of good sail cloth are as follows:

- It must be impermeable, which means that the cloth must be so tightly woven that the wind does not meet a porous, sieve-like surface but a continuous closed surface. The structure of the weave can be seen clearly under a magnifying glass. The separate threads of warp and weft, as the lengthwise and crosswise threads are called, must be so closely woven that you cannot see through them anywhere.

- The sail cloth should only stretch minimally under the pressure of the wind. This characteristic can be tested by pulling the cloth diagonally to the warp and weft, and you can then see how much the cloth deforms. Good cloth will only stretch slightly.

- Cloth that has been pulled out of shape must recover quickly and return to its original shape after stretching under load. The better the cloth is in this respect the longer will the original shape be maintained. The weight of the cloth is another important factor, for the heavier the cloth the more stable it will be. The weight of the sail cloth should be at least $4\frac{1}{2}$ oz ($3\frac{1}{2}$ oz in the US).

Sailors still have the idea that dyed sail cloth is not as good as white. This impression can be proved wrong in a laboratory test where values can be measured exactly. The decisive question is how the cloth is treated when being dyed. Depending on the technique employed it can be improved, made worse, or can remain equally good. Beware of judging sail cloth by its feel. Only experienced craftsmen can gauge quality in this way, and then only approximately.

The fact mentioned above that sails for Windsurfers have not conformed to the strict one design rule has been an advantage in some ways because, naturally, the earliest sails delivered before 1974 were not as good as those obtainable today. In particular, experience was lacking as to what was the most effective cut for sailboarding. The result is that, at the cost of not following the one design rules exactly, sails have been improved and a very good all purpose sail is now supplied.

The cut of today's Windsurfer sails will certainly be retained for many years. When the sail is set slackly a deep belly appears in the central part, and this disappears when tension is increased. As well as the position and depth of this fullness, the cut of the leech and the foot are very important. A well cut leech should not flutter, even in high winds, and this is also why battens are used to support the sail. Nor should the leech fall away to leeward because here, where the airflow breaks away, there must be a firm edge if the sail is to draw properly. A leech cut too round works equally inefficiently. The last inch or two of such a leech hooks up to windward instead of flowing smoothly aft, and because the leech will not open, even when the mast is very bent, the sail holds the wind like a paper bag. This makes it very difficult to sail a close hauled course, although there are certain slight advantages when the wind is free.

Similar problems can occur with the foot. If it flutters in strong winds it is not only disturbing after a time, but the shaking movement prevents good handling of the rig. On the other hand a foot cut too round is also to be avoided because the wind cannot flow away properly although, in this case, it can flow aft to the end of the boom.

Another major fault is when the fullness lies too far forward. The wishbone boom at that point is too narrow to accommodate the belly of the sail and cuts it into two parts. Nor can the air flow over the upper part of the sail properly, and the sail begins to shake aft of the mast. This shaking may become so violent that its disturbing influence affects the whole rig.

Rigging the Sailboard Correctly

Having considered all the important parts of the sailboard and explained the functions of the individual parts, we now come to the question of tuning the rig correctly. In sailing boats the expression tuning also includes the stepping of the mast in relation to the boat or, to put it better, in relation to the centre of lateral resistance. This aspect of tuning is a basic element of sailboarding technique in that the surfer continuously alters the position of the rig relative to the wind and to the centreline of the board. In addition he alters the CLR both by raising and lowering the daggerboard, and by moving his weight forward and aft on the surfboard.

So, when writing on the subject of tuning the surfboard's rig, we mean adjusting the sail with the luff downhaul, the outhaul and the inhaul. It is possible by increasing the tension to flatten the sail. The basic rule for this is: *use a full sail in light breezes and a flat sail in strong winds.*

The way to flatten the sail is simply to increase the tension of the luff downhaul which is connected to the mast foot and then follow by tightening the outhaul which is connected to the end of the wishbone boom until the sail is stretched to the very end of the boom. To make the sail fuller you only have to ease the tension on both lines. But be sure that you do not allow the sail to form a crease in the luff (i.e. immediately behind the mast sleeve).

When you are tensioning your sail and the wind is blowing strongly it is obvious that you cannot hold it up to windward but, as you can see in the first photograph, the wind itself raises the sail and this helps to make the job considerably easier. The next photograph shows how a full sail rests on the wishbone boom. You can also see how much it curves. The belly of the sail catches more air which is what is required in lighter winds. This sack-like effect disappears, however, when the sail is trimmed flat. The wind can then flow over the sail easily and the sailboarder does not need to use so much strength to support the rig. If the wind is blowing at over force 6 a storm sail should be used.

The inhaul line is tied to the mast with a rolling hitch. The rolling hitch must be pulled so tight that it cannot slip down even a fraction of an inch. It is a good idea to bind two or three turns of waterproof adhesive tape round the mast just below the point at which you like to attach your boom, so as to ensure that the inhaul cannot slip. After the sail has been sleeved over the mast the end of the inhaul has to be led through the eye of the boom back around the mast again, and then made fast to the cleat on the side of the boom. It is most important to ensure that two strands link mast to boom, as one alone will tend to stretch and loosen in use.

There is one disadvantage to the rolling hitch however. It is very bulky and the mast pockets of some sails, such as those of the new storm sails, are too narrow to enable the sail to be pulled down over the mast without first undoing the rolling hitch. In this case it is better to make a figure of eight knot in the end of the inhaul, lead it through the eye in the boom, take it twice round the mast, back through the eye and then make it fast to the cleat. The difficulty with this method is that the inhaul can slip down the mast and, in consequence, the gap in the sail pocket will probably tear in time because it has to take all the strain. This can be prevented easily enough by applying adhesive tape around the mast to stop the inhaul slipping down. It is especially advisable to do this is, as in surfing schools for example, many people of different heights use the same surfboard and the height of the boom has to be adjusted to suit them.

Before rigging the sailboard check carefully that the rolling hitch is tied on the mast at the correct height. As a general rule the boom should be attached to the mast at shoulder height. Sailboarders are often seen falling in just when raising the mast out of the water because the boom has been attached too low, and in consequence they are pulling at the wrong angle.

There is another important point in connection with attaching the boom to the mast. The essential requirement is that the mast should fit as closely as possible into the fork of the wishbone boom. The rig

cannot be controlled properly if there is too much play between them, and the inhaul will slap back and forth particularly in stronger winds. There is a simple way to ensure that you get a really snug fit here. Before cleating the inhaul lay the boom and the mast lengthwise on the ground, both pointing in the same direction. The mast and boom can then be lashed very tightly to each other. When the boom is lowered or, to put it better, is set at an angle of 90° to the mast, it will be found that the fit is very snug indeed.

Some sailboarding schools advise that the luff downhaul should be attached by a reef knot. We would like to make an alternative suggestion because, in our opinion, the essential point is not so much to teach as many specialized seamen's knots as possible, but rather to use those knots which are absolutely effective and as simple as possible so that they can be remembered easily.

The main consideration in the case of the luff downhaul is that it must be possible to apply tension to the mast in heavy winds without too much effort. What you need to be able to do is to bend the mast aft by increasing the tension of the luff downhaul. The

Peter Brockhaus demonstrates on the beach how the sail can be trimmed when it is blowing hard.

Here the sail is full as is required for light winds...

... and it is rigged flat for fresh winds on this Sea Panther. *Photo David Eberlin.*

three half hitches, and the sail will not give even a fraction of an inch.

Naturally the luff downhaul should not be tensioned more than is necessary. In winds of force 1 to 2 make it fast without tensioning it at all, but in winds of force 5 to 6 pull it as taut as you can. If no creases are to form the important point is that the tension of your sail should be about equal along the luff and the leech. If creases do appear the tension of both the luff downhaul and the outhaul should be adjusted.

Tension the sail to a greater or lesser degree according to the strength of the wind, and test the rig on land to see how well the sail is setting. If you are dissatisfied because there are too many creases in the sail alter the tension of both downhaul and outhaul.

Do not overdo your attempts to prevent creases forming because it is sometimes found that a sail with many creases draws better than a sail with none at all.

In any case your sailboard will never be a faultless 'sailing machine' with the rig tuned to perfection because your own body, the most important link between sailboard and rig, contributes so many shortcomings that one crease in the sail matters little. Before a race, or when surfing fast just for pleasure, it is much more worthwhile to get your own body into good trim by taking part in other sports or doing exercises which will improve your physical fitness. This is definitely a better way to prepare than to spend overmuch time fiddling around with your surfboard.

Checking your Equipment for Heavy Weather Sailing

After having read all the dry advice contained in the last sections the sailboarder who has bought his surfboard not just for sailing in winds of under force 4 but who is keen to do more than just gentle planing

downhaul should be attached to the eye on the sail with a bowline, and it is then led between the eye on the mast foot and the eye on the sail two or three times. This provides a simple purchase which will enable you to apply considerable tension to the sail without using excessive effort. Finish off with two or

about on inland waters should take a deep breath and concentrate on what follows. 'He who sows the wind reaps the storm' to apply a biblical quotation to sailboarding, and it is then a question of how much the sailboarder and his equipment can stand.

Some of the equipment that is manufactured today for sailboards is quite suitable for gentler breezes but is inadequate for winds of over force 4. The vital points which you must check without fail are these:

The sail Is your sail cut flat enough for strong winds? If it is too full the luff will pull on your hands like a pneumatic hammer and you will shoot up into the wind when you try to get under way.

Are all the seams in good condition? In particular keep an eye on the lower part of the mast sleeve. If the stitching is weak here you need only to fall into the sail once and it will tear up to the height of the boom.

Are the eyes strong enough? An eye that pulls out will unquestionably be the cause of your first damage. A good sail should be reinforced at least fourfold at the eyes with heavy sailcloth.

Mast foot Does the mast foot fit properly in the step in the sailboard? It should be neither too tight nor too loose. Have you rigged a safety line to secure the mast foot to the daggerboard? If the surfboard and the rig part company in winds of force 5 and over, the board will drift away much faster than you can swim, and this can occur in breaking surf as well.

Have you checked all the screws at the mast foot? A screwdriver is an indispensible tool to take with you in your sail bag.

You should also check the fittings on the boom regularly.

The snubber on the boom If your surfboard is one which is supplied without a snubber fitted to the boom, you should make one yourself. It is much cheaper and easier than having to mend a hole in the surfboard.

Reefing

Should conditions prove too strong for you to handle, there is a simple method of reefing, which can, if necessary, be carried out whilst on the water. Untie the luff downhaul line and push the bottom end of the sail sleeve up the mast as far as the boom inhaul, so that it is gathered as tightly as possible. Then tie the luff downhaul line to the inhaul or to the top of the boom.

The effect of this may look and feel a little peculiar, for there is now a loose bundle of sail gathered between the wishbone, with no sail at all below it. This puts about one third of the area of the sail out of commission, and you will find the balance of the rig has changed because the centre of effort has now moved higher up the sail.

Using a reefed sail *photo: London Sailboards*

Clothing

Another important consideration which affects both your safety and, naturally, your enjoyment when sailboarding is what you wear while you are sailing. There are quite a lot of firms that make clothing which is functionally suited to sailboarding, and we will therefore discuss the subject thoroughly because we want to avoid any possibility of your pleasure being lessened by badly cut clothing.

Special clothes are needed for sailboarding, just as they are needed for all other sports. Broadly speaking, if you will be sailing in waters with temperatures of over 68°F and where air temperatures are over 75°F you will find that swimming clothes are adequate. This is not the case in lower temperatures and you will then require protection against cold. The problem is that a garment designed to protect the body from cold, generally known as a wet suit, is usually made for a diver and is unsuitable for a sailboarder. The essential factor so far as neoprene clothing is concerned is that it must fit very closely to the body.

Warmth results from the fact that only a thin film of water or damp can lie between skin and clothing, and this film is warmed by body heat. If the distance between your skin and the neoprene clothing is too great the principle of insulation no longer functions. Cold water can find its way in, at the collar for instance, and spread over the whole body. It runs along the creases in the clothing to other parts of the body as if it were channelled, and the result is not so much protection against cold as a cooling system. Unfortunately some firms' only solution to the sailboarders' problem has, until now, been to cut surfing clothing over-generously. Equally it is quite evident that too closely fitting wet suits are not a good solution either because they cut into the shoulders and constrict the arm muscles, both of which are bad faults.

Neoprene is not just neoprene. It is available in good and poor qualities, and this is true not only of the nylon lining but also of the foam itself. Good surfing clothing must be made of very soft and flexible neoprene so that the close-fitting suit does not constrict the muscles. It is advisable to check too that the small air bubbles on the inner side of the neoprene foam are sealed, because you need only to warm your body and not the rubber as well. These air bubbles are important, however, as they give the garment buoyancy.

Most of today's clothing is lined with nylon fabric on both sides, both because it looks better and because the lining protects the neoprene from being damaged by sharp objects. This is not the right answer for sailboarders however because the nylon lining slips too easily on the finely roughened surface where you stand on the sailboard. Smooth black neoprene, or the material called shark skin, is preferable and a considerable improvement in this respect. You will probably be asking now 'Why should my surfing clothing be non-slip — the main

A team from the German magazine *Windsurfing* modelling a wide variety of surfing clothing.

essential is that I have a sure foothold'. This is certainly true in normal sailboarding, but not when it comes to breaking surf or sailing in very strong winds when you will be sitting or kneeling on the sailboard, not only just before you start but also when under way.

Anyone can see for himself by looking through typical sailboarding photographs which details of surfing clothing have to be cut differently to a diver's wet suit. Legs, like skiers' legs, are generally bent while arms and shoulders are bent and stretched powerfully. The sailboarder often stands with his legs far apart or kneels on one knee with the other leg stretched out. The critical points, therefore, are shoulders, elbows, biceps, forearms, and you must be able to kneel and stretch your legs far apart.

When buying clothing for sailboarding be sure that it fits particularly well at these places. You often see sailboarders who have cut the arms off their neoprene clothing because the suit stopped the blood flowing or was too tight and stiff. It is absolutely essential to have zips along the forearms or velcro fastening which is better still because it can be adapted more easily to the individual. Gussets where the knees and elbows bend are normally unnecessary unless the neoprene is particularly inflexible. Remember in this connection that, basically, unlined neoprene is more flexible than lined because nylon stretches very little.

Good surfing clothing should be suitable for a wide range of temperatures because otherwise you will freeze or sweat. Lately the longjohn has been used most widely for sailboarding. It protects the whole body except the arms from cold water and wind, and therefore gives maximum freedom of movement in the arm region. Short or long jackets can be used on colder days. Some sailboarders do without such jackets and, to give greater freedom to their arms in cold weather, wear woollen angora shirts instead, or neoprene vests with an anorak on top, like skiers.

The decisive factor when choosing a wetsuit is the thickness of the neoprene, and we suggest that at the cold time of the year at least 5mm is required to protect you against cold. This means either buying one set of 5mm clothing or a 3mm set plus a 2mm set. The latter method means that you have clothing for the in-between periods and for the summer, and two suits will not necessarily be all that much more expensive. Two layers of clothing on top of each other also improve insulation because a second film of water is built up between them. Given material of the same quality two thinner suits are also more flexible than one thick one.

These basic ideas are enough for now. Remember that you should always feel comfortable in your clothing and, above all, that it must keep you warm.

The same is true of footwear too. First and foremost it should keep your feet warm because cold feet lead to shaky legs and you should not then be surprised if you fall into the water constantly. Several firms make special shoes for sailboarders, but not all of them can be recommended. The essential points when it comes to sailboarding shoes are as follows:

- They must keep the feet really warm.
- They must have non-slip soles which are suited to the standing surface of your sailboard.
- The soles must make it possible for you to control the sailboard properly. They must not be too thick, nor should they catch the sides of your feet.
- They must be easy to pull on and off.

A good alternative, if nothing better can be found, is to use gym shoes over warm neoprene socks.

In the autumn, when the water is still warm but the first cold fronts bring cooler winds, warm gloves are absolutely essential because you cannot hold onto the boom for long without them. Do not just take any old pair of gloves that seems suitable, but buy a pair of neoprene gloves with chamois leather palms.

They must fit closely without creasing and have strong velcro fastening at the wrist to prevent them being pulled off gradually.

Dressed like this you can even sail in cold winter weather when sailors have already long since laid up their boats. The spectators on land will ask themselves how you can bear to be out there because they do not know how warm you can be when you are sailboarding in answer to the challenge of the wind.

The HiFly board.

Getting Under Way in Strong Winds

When you are sailboarding in force 1—3 you glide gently and noiselessly over the water, and this gives particular pleasure to advanced sailors as well. Surfing in fresh or strong winds above force 4, however, is absolutely intoxicating and everybody who has reached this stage in sailboarding is affected in the same way. You suddenly become wind-conscious. Even at home or when out walking you watch the leaves move to the wind and wonder whether it is blowing strongly enough for body-dip, when the body touches the water.

The man who goes out in fresh winds for the first time must expect to fall in again and again, just like a beginner, and this will also happen later on when, after some time, he dares to test himself in a stronger wind yet. The same difficulties that cause beginners to despair in winds of force 4 will be experienced even by the world champion in forces 8, 9 and 10. The explanation of strong wind technique which follows is therefore valid, with certain limitations, for the whole range of the Beaufort scale because there is no longer any doubt that the sailboard is a craft that is seaworthy even in a hurricane, always provided that the sailor has sufficient knowledge and courage, as well as the right sail. Force 6 to 7 is the absolute limit for a normal racing sail, but you can still sailboard in force 7 to 8 with a smaller sail.

For this reason the first important rule before starting should be, to check first whether the wind is already blowing too hard for the large sail. In this case use your storm sail.

The second important rule, to which reference will often be made but which cannot be too heavily stressed for beginners is: *never start sailboarding in fresh or strong winds if the wind is blowing from the land*. The only exception is when you are sailing on a small lake and will quickly finish up on the opposite shore.

Before we start to consider the theory and practise of sailboarding in strong winds, the basic difference between a sailing boat and a sailboard must be made quite clear. The two photographs show this clearly.

The first photograph is of a sailboard with the mast strongly inclined to windward, while the other shows a sailing boat heeling.

It is an extraordinary fact that the aspects of sailboarding which strike spectators as strange are that the sailboarder stands up when he sails, and that he stands on a board. People fail to notice that in increasing winds a sailboard is sailed with the mast inclined to windward, whereas the mast of a sailing boat leans to the opposite side — to leeward. The second difference is that the sailboard itself still remains horizontal on the water when the mast is inclined, whereas the sailing boat heels to leeward too, and can even capsize to leeward.

Beginners are unaccustomed to this: in fresh winds the mast of the sailboard is inclined to windward. . .

...whereas that of a sailing boat inclines to leeward.

In the beginners' part of this book we have already pointed out a third important difference which is that the sailboard is steered by raking the mast forward and aft. It will now become clear that, when sailing a sailboard, the ability to incline the mast to windward is equally important. This is particularly true during the starting phase in heavy weather. If we revert first to the theory of how the sailboard changes direction we remember that, when tacking, the mast is inclined aft just above the water and the board. The closer the sail is to the water, the faster will the sailboard turn into the wind. Conversely, the further the foot of the sail is from the surface of the water, the slower will the sailboard tack or luff up to windward. The awkward tendency that the sailboard has of luffing up in strong winds can only be avoided if the foot of the sail and the end of the boom point upwards as steeply as possible. In the starting phase in strong winds the foot can only point upwards if the mast is inclined far to windward. You may perhaps wonder why it is not inclined forward as you have learnt when bearing away. The reason is that the wind would immediately whip the sail out of your hands as soon as you attempted to harden it, however slightly. Furthermore your weight would have to be placed very far forward which would overload the bow of the sailboard, and this makes it more likely to cut under the waves.

Pulling the mast over to windward has the effect of reducing the projected sail area, that is, the amount of sail area offered to the wind. This reduces the pressure of the wind on the sail and not so much strength is required to support the rig. When sailboarding with the sail pulled over to windward above you the almost horizontal position of the sail gives rise to lift in the same way as does an aeroplane's wing. This force acting upwards lifts part of the weight of the sailboard and the sailboarder, and this again reduces the amount of strength required.

Before we look at the separate stages of getting under way we can already see clearly the main point to be remembered: when getting under way in strong winds, incline the mast well to windward to avoid luffing up.

Sailing in breaking surf calls for considerable skill and excellent balance.

The Individual Stages

Even raising the sail from the water presents problems in high winds, but it can be made easier if the uphaul is pulled not merely towards the body but slightly towards the bow with a swinging movement of the mast hand so that the water can flow off the leech of the sail. As soon as the pressure eases raise the rig by pulling firmly with both hands, grasping the knots in the uphaul. Remember your beginner's course: your legs are stronger than your arms, so bend your knees before pulling up the sail and help to raise the rig by straightening your legs.

When you have raised the sail you must take care that the end of the boom does not again come into contact with the water because the wind will then immediately thrust the sail down into it again.

Here is another important point for heavy weather and in breaking surf. You will sometimes find that your sail is pushed deep under the water by a wave or by the wind. This does not make things any more difficult provided that the mast is still lying on the surface of the water, and may even make it easier because, by pulling back on the mast, you may be able to get the sail to lie pointing downwards beneath the water, and it can be raised from this position without difficulty.

The board will generally luff up sharply while you are raising the rig. You will be so preoccupied that you will not notice this at first, but it is extremely important in fresher winds that you turn the board back to the starting position with the wind abeam. In strong winds it is easier to start even from a position with the wind free than with the board in a close hauled position.

Before moving your mast hand from the uphaul and catching hold of the boom over the other hand, take a good step towards the stern until your weight is aft of the daggerboard slot, and also bring your forward foot further aft, roughly between the mast foot and the daggerboard slot. Crouch slightly because you are about to assume a very unstable stance to which you are completely unaccustomed. First grasp the boom with the mast hand about 8 inches aft of the mast and incline the rig to windward, pointing towards the wind. As you do this you will turn your torso towards the sail so that the wind no longer comes from behind you but from the side. Make sure that your sail is still shaking freely in the wind. Now catch hold of the boom with your aft hand a good distance away from the mast hand so that you get good leverage. This position is also quite strange to you because the sail prevents you seeing forward in the direction in which you will be sailing, and is especially awkward in the case of those sailboard sails that have only one window.

Starting in strong winds.
1. Once you are standing up with the sail flapping
2. Pull the mast well over to windward
3. Harden the sail and bend the knees. Push the board forward with the feet.
4. The start was successful.

94

The moment at which you gather way calls for great concentration. The sail hand on the wishbone boom hardens the sail a fraction until slight pressure from the wind can be felt, and the board gradually starts to make way. If the pressure is too strong ease the sail immediately. Try this slight hardening of the sail several times to get some practice. Once you are making way as a result of hardening the sail gently like this the pressure on it will ease slightly and you will then be able to harden rather more. Continue hardening in stages in this way until you have gathered full way. It is best to crouch quite low so that the centre of gravity of your body is as close as possible to the water, and to push the sailboard forward with your legs. This method of hardening the sail gradually means that you do not suddenly have to counter the pressure of the wind by the weight of your body but can slowly and gradually get into the sailing position.

You will be surprised at how soon you can master the art of getting under way in strong winds if you are careful about the following points:

- Incline the mast a long way to windward before grasping the boom with your sail hand.
- Place your feet directly forward and aft of the daggerboard slot.
- Remember that it is easier to get under way from a beam reach or a broad reach.
- Harden the sail progressively and crouch low, pushing the board forward with your feet.

A particularly thrilling method of getting under way will be described in the section on sailboarding without a daggerboard. Here it need only be said that the exertion required when getting under way in

Raising the sail in a strong wind; this often causes problems. If the right technique is used it can be done without too much effort. Important — as soon as the rig has been partly raised continue to pull it up rapidly until the sail is right out of the water.

strong winds naturally also depends on the inertia of the sailboard.

Because the daggerboard presents most resistance it is easier and quicker to get under way with it slightly raised, provided that you have no difficulties with your balance. As a second step in learning how to get under way in strong winds practise with the daggerboard raised slightly. You will find this technique becomes necessary as soon as the wind increases further.

Another extremely effective and worthwhile way of practising is to try to stay for as long as possible in the position when you have both hands on the boom but are not under way. You just let the sail shake while keeping the mast inclined far to windward. Also practise altering the direction in which your sailboard is pointing by making quite small corrections, hardening, easing and backing the sail. This will be very useful later, not only before the start of a race but also in breaking surf when you want to wait for an especially attractive formation of waves. When you are in this position you are ready to get under way immediately.

When starting in a strong wind set off with determination, pulling the rig over to windward and using all your weight.

Body-Dip and Head-Dip

Body-dip and head-dip are among the most advanced skills of sailboarding, particularly when they are performed rhythmically at regular intervals. It is useful to prepare for body-dip by first surfing in a very deep crouch with your body close above the water. Your arms are fully stretched and keep the wind pressure on the sail and the weight of your body in a state of equilibrium. Your legs are far apart, and forward leg slightly bent towards the direction in which you are sailing, while the aft leg is well bent at right angles to the centre line.

First of all cover longer stretches in this position, sweeping low over the water and sailing effortlessly and completely relaxed. The sail hand eases the sail as and when the wind becomes too strong.

Try to touch the water when you are close hauled.

Body dip; almost an acrobatic feat. After your back touches the water your sail hand must harden the sail so that the wind can raise both you and the rig.

The sailboard and sail are most stable when you are on this course and you can use the waves formed by the wind. Let yourself fall into the next large wave and harden the sail at the same moment. The increased pressure on the sail will soon lift you up again. If there is not quite sufficient wind you can nevertheless avoid falling by bending your knees quickly. This is called knee thrust and is an action which must be mastered because it is often your only way of countering a sudden lull in the wind and so avoiding a fall. A knee thrust brings the centre of gravity of the body over the board lightning fast and the state of equilibrium is recovered.

Matching rhythmic body-dip to the pattern of waves is most rewarding as the crest of every wave is touched by your body. Raising and lowering your body is the best practice for increasing your endurance when sailboarding. A skilled sailboarder can virtually bring the board to a halt by totally immersing his body in a wave. This is also a preparatory step for one of the hardest tricks in sailboarding, starting from the water. When you start in this way you let yourself fall completely into the water and are raised by the sail while your feet, in the meanwhile, have no contact whatsoever with the sailboard.

When you are immersed in a wave while the board is sailing flat out, board speed is cut virtually to nothing and the apparent wind will change sharply to coincide with the true wind. It will then strike the close hauled sail from abeam and raise it, even if the mast is pulled over very far to windward.

In the case of *head-dip*, as the term implies it is the

head and not the body which touches the water. The principle is the same as that of body-dip. Sail close hauled, luff up while you are hanging close over the water, then hollow your back and touch the water with your head. At the same time harden the sail with your sail hand and the pressure on it will be enough to raise you again. While you are doing this you cannot see at all where you are going, so you must know beforehand whether there is enough sea room for you to enjoy head-dip. It is more difficult than with a body-dip to control the hardening and easing of the sail without altering course violently. If you luff too far when touching the water and shoot up to windward the angle of attack becomes too acute and the wind cannot lift you up again. Therefore, with body-dip as with head-dip, you should incline the mast slightly further forward at the same moment as you harden the sail, the principle being that when you touch the water the board will already be bearing away and you will be raised by the acceleration which results from bearing away.

European champion Derk Thijs on a run. He is almost lying on the board.

Sailboarding is a highly photogenic Sport. This photograph was awarded a prize when the first sailboarding photographic competition was run.

The Jump Tack

In the meanwhile your practising will have enabled you to make a great deal of progress. A wind of force 4 to 5 is nothing to worry about any more and, on the contrary, now gives you great pleasure. This is the moment to polish up your tacking.

First let us remember what we learnt in the basic course. Tacking is initiated by inclining the mast aft or, as we have just said in relation to getting under way in stronger winds, by pulling the foot over the water towards the stern. The nearer the foot of the sail is to the surface of the water the easier will the sailboard turn towards the wind. When the bow of the board is heading directly into the wind you take small steps to move round the mast and, while supporting the rig by the uphaul, complete the tack by pressing the sail against the wind. The completion can be said to be a new start because you are back in your basic position again, with the sail supported by the uphaul and your legs to left and right of the mast foot. We will now consider this simple method of tacking in very restricted water, and particularly when the wind is blowing hard.

We are sailing flat out on a beam reach! It is best to select two buoys to tack round, and ideally they should be about 100 yards apart. The mast is inclined slightly to windward. We sail about two yards to leeward of the buoy and, when we are level with it, pull the sail aft with a hefty tug. At the same time we take a good step aft so as to shift the weight of the body towards the stern. The board immediately shoots up into the wind, and so rapidly that you must try to get forward with a small jump or two quick steps. You then have to stand forward of the mast until the board has turned right through the wind. A second determined jump now brings you back to your new sailing position. With a sweeping movement incline the sail forward towards the bow and also pull it over to windward and then, off you go, back to the other buoy.

The jump tack should first be practised making two

separate jumps. With your first you half turn your body as you jump to a position forward of the mast and, ideally, your toes should be pointing aft on either side of the mast foot when you land. The second jump is from this position to the new sailing position, and again your body makes a half turn.

When you have mastered the jump tack to some extent you can attempt to go about with only one jump. This, however, can only be achieved when the board has swung so far before you jump that it has passed well through the eye of the wind.

The description sounds impossibly acrobatic, but when you look at it more closely it is not really quite so impossible to get round the mast with only one jump because the board turns virtually on a sixpence as a result of inclining the rig to windward of the centreline of the sailboard.

When the board has achieved full turning momentum your body actually only needs to make a half turn in the air because the board itself continues to turn and will be beneath your feet when you land. The essential thing is to choose the right moment to jump. If you wait too long the pressure on the sail drops away completely and you fall to windward beneath it. If you jump too early you land near the sailboard rather than on it because it has not turned completely through the wind.

This method of doing a jump tack is certainly one of the most difficult feats to attempt when sailboarding and the man who has really mastered it can consider himself an expert. Strictly speaking it is pure show, like body-dip and head-dip, because you lose almost all way and risk falling. This is why the jump tack is rarely used when racing. There are awkward moments which occur over right of way situations, however, when a quick jump tack has distinct advantages. We also feel that everything that relates to show is as much a part of our sport as the wind. So, practise the jump tack — it will give you more pleasure than it gives to the people watching from the shore.

Finally, another problem that arises primarily when going about in a strong wind. We omitted it earlier so as not to make the jump tack appear over-complicated. You may well have found sometimes when going about that your mast hand was forced to let go

The jump tack is the quickest way to alter course.

of the boom because the pressure was too great. What was the cause? The answer is that you have hardened the sail faster than the board was luffing to windward, and the wind — in this case the true wind blowing from further aft than the apparent wind — has suddenly caught the sail and torn it from your hand. You have overdone it, or possibly even let the mast tilt to leeward.

How can you prevent this happening? It is quite simple. When you are tacking you must get into the habit of inclining the mast both aft and to windward as well. This is a very unnatural sequence of movement which you can try out with your eyes closed now, while you are reading this book. Your arms are stretched out about 2ft 6in apart. Bring your mast hand back quite close to your body while keeping your sail hand fully stretched but swinging downwards. This can be easily and effectively practised on land or on the simulator.

Here the mast is inclined far aft and the sail pulled well over. The jump tack will follow immediately.

The Stop Gybe

The opposite to the jump tack could be said to be the stop gybe, to a certain extent. This too can be, or rather should be just as fast and may be used where there is little searoom. It is neither as elegant nor as satisfying as the jump tack, and is also a good deal more difficult if the wind is strong. Nevertheless it is something which astonishes all sailors when compared with gybing a sailing boat. What actually happens when you gybe a sailboard?

You know already that, to gybe, you swing the sail over the bow. This is nothing new for advanced sailors, but what you probably did not notice when doing your first gybe was that something happened which is quite exceptional for a winddriven craft; you could stop your sailboard on the spot. To express it differently, from every point of sailing you can bring your board to a halt at lightning speed by using a stop gybe. This immediately tells us when the stop gybe is especially useful — when giving way in an emergency situation. Naturally every beginner also knows the proven method of stopping by just letting the mast fall into the water, but although this method is effective it is hardly elegant. Let us look at the stop gybe more closely.

Every other sailing craft must shoot up into the wind in order to stop. Not so a sailboard sailor who, on whatever point of sailing he may be, can pull the rig round over the bow and against the wind, thus braking his speed immediately.

How does this stop gybe work? Imagine that you are sailing with the wind abeam and that, suddenly, an obstacle appears ahead. Before starting the stop gybe you must bend your arms so that you are in full control. Then the sail hand moves forward close to the mast hand which lets go of the boom and catches hold of it again on the opposite side, close to the mast. Immediately afterwards the sail hand grasps the uphaul, while the mast hand pulls the rig towards the wind and as low over the bow of the sailboard as possible. This causes way to be lost immediately and the board begins to turn. The legs are used to encourage the turning movement. As soon as you are standing on the new windward side you revert to the starting position and harden the sail. If a stop gybe is well executed the surfboard will stop on the spot with no way on, and in a new starting position at that, ready to get under way again.

1. The stop gybe. From under way, close hauled . . .
2. suddenly back the sail . . .
3. turn the bow beneath the sail . . .
4. until the board is on the other tack and then get under way again.

Running

When sailboarding the run is not only the slowest point of sailing — and this is true of all sailing boats — but is also the least stable and the most difficult. This could be said to be a good reason for spending as little time as possible on the run, but it is an interesting and challenging point of sailing nevertheless, especially in a seaway and in stronger winds. Once the basic groundwork on the principle of running has been assimilated you will soon come to appreciate the especial pleasures of downwind work.

A sail with three windows is absolutely essential. It is true that for may years sailboards have managed to get by without the new three-window sails, but, nowadays, no-one would like to do without the advantages they bring and be forced to sail as blindly as was inevitable when sails had only one window. Before you can get onto a run you first have to be able to bear away and, in fresh winds, bearing away is the most common cause of falls. Catapult falls, capsize falls and diving falls, which are covered in the next chapter, all have to be taken into account and avoided as far as possible by taking the correct action.

When you bear away in fresh winds you must start to do so very carefully. The mast, which is pulled over to windward, has to be inclined slightly further forward while, at the same time, the sail hand carefully hardens the sail but is always ready to ease it out again if the wind pressure becomes excessive. As soon as the sailboard starts to bear away the sail hand eases the sail and continues to do so until the board is sailing dead before the wind. A wide-spread fault among sailboarders is that, because it is difficult to bear away, they use the forward foot too firmly to help the sailboard to turn. In consequence there is a danger that the board may cut under the waves due to excessive weight on the forward foot, and the final result may well be a case of 'diving stations'. Get into the habit of gybing with the sail and not by using your feet. When you are gybing do not let your foot try to creep forward of the mast. Place it near the mast and

put only as much weight on it as is required to keep the weight of your body properly balanced in relation to the sailboard because a board with the weight too far aft will obviously be more difficult to gybe. If you do not have an extra window to allow you to take up the low hanging stance confirm beforehand that there are no craft to leeward with which you could collide.

You have to survive a particularly critical phase when the air suddenly ceases to flow over the sail with the result that the wind pressure decreases so much that you can easily lose your balance. In view of this, when you are bearing away you have to bring the centre of gravity of your body over the surfboard before the airflow ceases. It is best to kneel on the surfboard on your left leg, while your forward leg stays stretched out. Alternatively you can use knee thrust as we have already described to bring your centre of gravity over the board. Which method you use will depend on whether you will be crouching, standing or kneeling when you are sailing on the run.

Your choice of position will be governed by how many windows there are in your sail. If you have only one window you have no choice and will have to stand because your eyes must be at the height of the window if you are going to be able to see ahead of the board.

The most stable position is if you keep your legs apart with one foot near the daggerboard slot pointing forward and the other aft of the slot pointing athwartships so that you can balance the board better. This is advisable in strong winds in particular when the following waves tend to push the board from one side to the other.

When you are standing your position is very unstable because it is so difficult to counter any gusts that strike the sail. You can easily be pulled forward off

Kneeling on a run . . .

112

balance and your sail hand then has to let go. This means that you will then have to make a running start, and this is one of the most difficult things to attempt when the wind is fresh.

If you are to be at all steady when you are standing up and a gust strikes you, bend your elbows so that the increase in pressure can be absorbed first by straightening your arms, and you will then have enough time to react with a knee thrust. What we are trying to explain here will best be understood if you make a simple experiment at home. Stand upright with your legs in the position suggested, your front foot pointing forward and your back foot pointing at right angles to it. Your arms are well bent and you are holding the boom horizontally in front of you. Now imagine that a gust strikes from behind and tries to tear the sail from your hands. Thrust your knees forward and let your arms give to the pressure. Then try to do the same when your feet are side by side and close together. You can test your reactions by holding a broom handle in your hands with a piece of rope attached to it. Get someone to pull the rope hard and without warning, and ask him to try to pull you off balance.

Next try the kneeling position, kneeling on one leg while the other one is stretched forward. You will find that it is almost impossible to be pulled over. Your centre of gravity will be lying close above the surfboard, and even a very strong pull from ahead cannot unbalance you. It is also much easier to balance the unsteady surfboard on a run when you are kneeling. Practise this position at home and you will be surprised at how easy the next run will seem.

The only times that you will crouch are when you will be on a run for a very short period, for example when gybing. Make a point of practising changing the position of your feet because they only stay beside

... and Gordon Way demonstrates railriding downwind on a Sea Panther. *Photo David Eberlin.*

each other for a short while during a gybe.

With a view to feeling really at home with your sailboard, and for sheer pleasure as well, you should try the sitting and lying down positions when running. They are nothing like as difficult as they appear to be, provided that you try them first in winds of force 3—4. In very strong winds the lying position may well be the only way in which you can sail a run because it is only like this that you can project and support a small enough area of sail. Practising these extreme positions is also useful later, and particularly when sailing in breaking surf, because you may find that the waves tear your feet away from beneath you, and you suddenly find yourself sitting or lying down unintentionally. You would then already have experience of getting to your feet again.

To conclude this section we will add a few words on running in a seaway. We will concentrate first on the most normal situation which is running with waves raised by the wind overtaking from aft. In such conditions the best method is to let your board run freely without trying to correct every alteration to your course. One wave may push you to starboard while the next one pushes you to port and cancels out the

Helgo Lass, an expert in strong winds, makes himself comfortable lying down . . .

... but it is certainly not as easy as he makes it look, as here in force 6 winds.

effect of the first. Your aim is to use the thrust of the waves to best advantage. As soon as the seas become higher and you start real wave-riding you must raise the daggerboard slightly. By this time, of course, you will be surfing in the original sense of the word in that it is no longer the inclination of the sail which decides the direction in which the sailboard moves, but how you have placed the board and, naturally, the position of the daggerboard. In real wave-riding you use your feet while the sail is used very little or not at all. The daggerboard is merely a hindrance because the directional stability which it provides keeps the board straight on its original course and makes it very much more difficult to turn the sailboard with your feet or to drift with the waves. At first raise the daggerboard half way up its case; later models are pivoted, which makes it easier than pulling it upwards.

You will find that it is much easier to sail a fast run in strong winds like this. Later you can also try surfing without a daggerboard at all, as described on p.132. The run is a particularly difficult point of sailing in the open sea on those occasions when waves roll in from abeam or at an angle from astern. It is then better to sail a zig-zag course, first making maximum use of each individual wave and then regaining ground to windward so as not to be pushed too far off course by the waves.

Typical Falls in Strong Winds

Up to now when you fell you just fell. You did not notice any difference between your falls and only knew that you had landed in the water yet again. Sometimes you really enjoyed the feeling of flying through the air, but it was often discouraging too because you did not have the slightest idea as to why you had fallen. We are now going to study closely the typical falls that occur in strong winds, and learn how to avoid them.

Cutting Under the Waves and Diving Falls

When considering this way of falling we must first find out what is responsible for the sailboard cutting under the waves. There are sailboards that are so prone to nose-diving that only very good and very lightweight surfers can avoid a fall. As has already been explained, a sailboard which has this tendency usually suffers from inadequate sheer: the bow does

In a diving fall the braking effect is so great that the sailboarder is swung up in a steep curve.

not curve up enough. On the other hand, if your board is well curved forward the fault which leads to the fall is bound to lie in your own sailing technique. The most common failing is to bear away incorrectly, with one foot placed forward of the mast, pushing the surfboard away from the wind as hard as possible while, at the same time, the fact that the sail is there to be used for steering is forgotten completely.

Falling needs practise too. If the sailboarder is fit a leap like this can be changed into a skilful gymnastic exercise.

As soon as you get used to catching hold of the boom rather further aft than usual you find that you can move the centre of effort of the sail further forward relatively easily without transferring your weight forward at the same time. It is then much easier to bear away and help is no longer needed from your feet. In any case when you are sailing on a fast broad reach your foot should be on the windward edge of the board so that you are correctly placed to prevent a capsize fall. If the board does start to cut under due to an awkward series of waves you must ease the sail immediately and shift your weight to the leeward side of the sailboard. This is the quickest way to get the sailboard clear of the water again and pointing close to the wind. You may possibly even manage to avoid a diving fall in this way.

If you do not ease the sail but just hope that the board will lift of its own accord you will induce a proper diving fall. The surfboard then continues to dive deeper until the time comes when you fall yourself. Diving falls are most likely to occur in breaking surf when you sail down a wave at great speed but fail to lose way in the trough.

The Capsize Fall

A few years ago, when the word sailboarding was rarely heard in Europe, you could often read in leaflets and newspaper or magazine articles that 'a Windsurfer cannot capsize'. We had gathered a good deal of experience of sailboarding, but no one had actually managed to capsize a sailboard, always excepting the fact that it is possible for a beginner to make a sailboard turn turtle when he makes the wrong movements.

We were used to explaining to interested bystanders: 'The mast of a sailboard can be inclined in any direction because of the universal joint. This causes the position of the mast to change continuously in relation to the board and also means that the sailboard cannot heel in the way that a sailing boat heels, but instead always lies flat on the water.'

Our first great surprise came when we had to sail back to the shore in a wind which was freshening rapidly. It was the first time that we had to deal with a wind of over force 5.

Suddenly it happened. The windward edge of the board lifted high and we could feel that the board was turning over round its fore-and-aft axis. Even 160 lbs of body weight placed on the edge of the board could not push it down. The result of this lifting

A capsize fall at its most extreme. Not everyone can manage to keep his stance on the side of the board as this sailboarder has done. Will he be able to force the board down again?

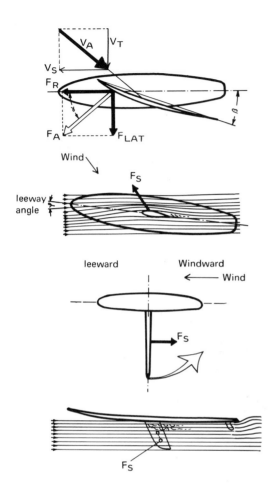

Clearly there had to be some connection with the actual speed of the board because capsize falling only occurred when we were sailing at our highest speeds. Obviously hydrodynamics and the theory of the flow of water past the sailboard and daggerboard played a considerable part.

Let us first look at the top drawing which shows the point of sailing on which most time is spent — close hauled. The aerodynamic force (F_A) generated by the action of the wind on the sail not only draws the sailboard forward in the direction of the course being sailed (driving force F_R) but also drives it sideways at right angles to the course (F_{lat}, lateral force). In consequence the sailboard makes some leeway and the water does not flow directly along the fore-and-aft axis of the board but at an acute angle to it from forward.

This slight angle of attack or leeway angle of the water flow at the daggerboard generates a side force (F_S) which acts to windward and opposes those forces which act laterally, pushing the board to leeward.

Without going into further detail about the theory of water flow, the important point here is that the lift or side force generated by the daggerboard increases when the speed of the water flowing past the board increases, or to put it in other words, when the sailboard sails faster through the water.

When this lift becomes excessive the sailboard will capsize to leeward around its fore-and-aft axis. The daggerboard is forced up to the surface of the water to windward and this throws the board and the surfer over. Other minor effects also contribute to the rotating movement.

- Due to the increased speed the bow of the board is lifted further above the water and this results in a reduction in longitudinal stability which is governed by the length of the surfboard on the water.

and turning movement was an unintentional fall into the water. The sailboard had capsized and it was lying on the water with the daggerboard pointing upwards. We could not conceive how such a fall was possible — we had been sailing quite normally and were not aware of having made any mistakes or incorrect movements.

More falls of the same type followed and we gradually realised that this phenomenon was not caused by wrong handling of the sailboard alone.

• The hydrodynamic lift or side force generated by the daggerboard is concentrated low down because it is pushed down by turbulence near the daggerboard slot, and this effectively increases the length of the lever arm.

How can a capsize fall be avoided? The obvious answer is not to sail so fast, but this is naturally an unsatisfactory solution. Board speed itself is the basic cause of capsize falling, if you except other minor contributory factors.

You will generally avoid capsize falling if you reduce the speed of the board, either by luffing up or by easing out the sail. This generally means that you will have to sail a zig-zag course which is certainly not the shortest distance between two points.

Of course you must always keep your feet on the windward edge of the board and use all the weight of your body there if you feel that you are starting to daggerboard plane, which is the term used to describe the lifting of the daggerboard to windward. You should also try to prevent the bow lifting too much when the sailboard accelerates and so ensure that the centres of effort and lateral resistance remain in a state of equilibrium. The effectiveness of all these suggestions is limited, however, and a capsize fall can only really be avoided if the daggerboard is removed or replaced by a smaller one which acts further aft.

Anyone who has seen a 21ft 4in Windglider-Tandem weighing 108 lbs capsizing or has himself capsize fallen with a Tandem will have some idea of the power of the lift generated by the daggerboard at speeds of over 15 knots.

Generally speaking raising the daggerboard half way is enough to avoid a capsize fall. This shortens the lever arm and the hydrodynamic lift generated at the daggerboard is reduced to such an extent that it is almost impossible to capsize. Naturally the board will be even more stable if the daggerboard is removed entirely because then daggerboard planing is quite impossible.

To summarize the facts that have been explained above: the faster you sail with the daggerboard down, the less stable the board will be, but the faster you sail without the daggerboard, the more stable the sailboard will become.

World champion Matt Schweitzer shows his skill and is completely relaxed on a beam reach. The daggerboard pulled up half way makes a capsize fall less likely and also increases the speed of the board.

The Catapult Fall

Undoubtedly the catapult fall is the most spectacular way of leaving the sailboard. You can see in the photograph that it can be a pleasure and, in consequence, you would be wise not only to learn how to avoid it but also how to master the art of catapult falling because it is a very safe way to fall.

Avoid a catapult fall in races and on those occasions when it ceases to be a pleasure:

• In water which is dirty or too cold.
• In shipping channels and off port entrances.
• In breaking surf when the seas are high.

What causes a catapult fall? The first essential for a real catapult fall is a force 4—5 wind. You start sailing with the wind abeam and the board moving fast because the sail is drawing well. You then alter course to a broad reach by bearing away slightly. The mast is inclined to windward, the sail hand hardens the sail gently and the body straightens up a little so that body weight is not concentrated too far aft on the board.

And already it has happened; a slight increase in the wind or a gust is all that is needed and you cannot hold on any longer — you fly through the air. All of a sudden the mast will have been jerked towards the bow, and so quickly that there is no time to react by letting go. Your hands are still grasping the boom because you are still trying to counter the increase in pressure, but you are no longer able to do so. As if fired from a catapult your body is first spun round lengthwise and then lands in the water near the board.

It is certainly no exaggeration to say that there are good sailboarders who catapult fall without being able to do anything to prevent it and, generally speaking, they also do not really know what has led to this phenomenon, nor what happens to the sail. Above all an explanation is needed as to why, on one occasion, a catapult fall will be particularly violent, while at other times it does not occur at all. Certainly many people find out by experience that the catapult fall can be avoided by easing the sail at the right moment — but what is the right moment? If you ease the sail too soon you do not bear away at all, but if you ease it too late you are also too late to avoid falling. If you are to choose the right moment you need to know what forces are acting on the sail when the board is on a broad reach.

First we must make it quite clear that, when the board is reaching, the apparent wind which results from board speed and the true wind combined does

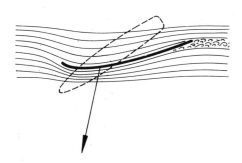
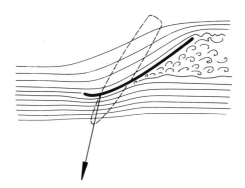

not flow only over the windward side of the sail but over the leeward side as well. Pressure is increased to windward, but is reduced to leeward.

The relationship between the two is depicted in the left hand drawing. The arrow from the leeward side of the sail indicates the direction and the strength of the aerodynamic force that the surfer has to counter. The sail has been drawn extending over the windward side of the surfboard, and this is to make it clear that, when there is a lot of wind, the mast is pulled over a long way to windward on this point of sailing.

The wind is dragging hard on the sail, and the water is far from calm. In such conditions it is extremely difficult to bear away and gradually alter course from the position shown on the left to that shown on the right.

Every experienced sailboarder knows that if he wants to bear away he not only inclines the mast further forward but also hardens the sail. We can now see what happens to the airflow on the leeward side of the sail when the board has borne away slightly and when, at the same time, the angle of attack of the wind at the sail becomes more acute.

In the drawing on the right the point of separation of the airflow to leeward can be seen to have moved far further forward and the force generated by the sail has also moved forward correspondingly, being concentrated in the forward part of the sail. The result is that the pull to be countered is both further to windward and further forward on the board.

This is the critical moment. In normal winds you would now ease out the sail and gradually alter course to a run, but the catapult fall does not occur in normal winds. Let us imagine ourselves in this situation in a fresh or strong wind of over force 5.

Just a wave, or the smallest wrong movement is enough to cause the airflow to break away, and when this happens the angle of pull jumps forward suddenly. The effect is naturally more marked if the sail has not been flattened sufficiently because it is then particularly difficult to control in high winds.

When the pulling force of the sail jumps forward in this way the forward hand alone suddenly has to counter all the pressure, but is not strong enough and cannot hold on any longer.

This change in the direction of the pulling force is complemented by a turning movement on the board which is due purely to the design of the surfboard. As you know, altering the centre of effort of the sail by inclining the mast further forward induces a turning movement which causes the board to bear away. The catapult fall is caused by the combination of the rapid jump forward of the pulling force of the sail with the turning movement of the board.

It quite often happens that the mast falls on the board, and if there is no snubber on the boom the result will generally be that the board is holed.

How can a catapult fall be avoided? It is easy enough to say that the answer is to use perfect technique when altering course, but there is no doubt that this is a great deal easier said than done. However, if you start practising in lighter winds and then gradually gain enough confidence to try in more wind you will have fewer problems with catapult falling.

When you are practising remember the following points:

- Always start gybing or bearing away much more carefully than when starting to make a tack. You can go about jerkily, but the start of a gybe must be smooth.
- The sail must be eased progressively as the board bears away. Only by doing this can you maintain proper airflow over the sail.
- In high winds ease the sail as follows: the sail hand eases the boom while, at the same time, the mast hand pulls the rig back towards the body. You

can also pull the mast further over to windward so as to keep the centre of effort of the sail forward. Basically, when bearing away bend your knees so that the centre of gravity of your body lies low, and you will not then be pulled forward off balance so easily.

The catapult fall, the most spectacular way of leaving the board, does have some hidden dangers. Remember the following points so that you get nothing but enjoyment from it.

- Never risk a catapult fall in busy waters or when ahead of another vessel.
- Confirm before you start to bear away onto a broad reach that you have searoom to leeward. If necessary sew additional windows into your sail.
- Above force 5 it is absolutely essential to tie a line between your daggerboard and the mast foot, for it is particularly likely that the foot of the mast will jump out of the step when catapult falling, and the sailboard will then drift away.

- If you should land immediately ahead of the board, protect your face with your hands. Should the boom land on the sailboard itself the board will not come to an immediate halt and could run onto your head.
- Catapult falls from the Tandem. Especial care is required in this case. The force on the sail work in exactly the same way as with a one-man sailboard. Therefore the aft man can be flung into the forward man which can be unpleasant on occasion. The forward man is particularly endangered if he lands ahead of the Tandem.

The higher speed and weight of the Tandem will at the very least leave you with a big lump on your head if you do not get out of the way quickly enough.

There is a general rule which must always be observed when sailing a Tandem: if one person falls the other must immediately let the rig drop into the water, to brake the sailboard to a halt. This is particularly important when it comes to a catapult fall.

Sailboards are no respecters of persons. HRH Prince Charles tries his hand off Cowes. *Photo Daily Telegraph.*

The greatest joys of sailboarding are experienced in the enormous waves off Hawaii. The intoxication of sailing down such waves has been experienced by only a few people.

Sailboarding in Breaking Surf

Watching a surfer rushing down the front of the waves in heavy breaking surf at fantastically high speeds fascinates all sailboarders. Sailboarding in the surf off Hawaii is a dream that can come true, but before daring to venture into such waters with a sailboard it is obviously sensible to start in the smaller breaking surf that can be found in northern Europe and in the Mediterranean where there are many more beaches with breakers than one would expect. If you heed the advice which follows you will find that it is a great deal easier than it looks.

An essential piece of equipment for sailing in breaking surf is a short daggerboard. As already explained on p.70 such a daggerboard has advantages in breaking surf.

- You can start or return to the shore in water that is shallower and the daggerboard slot is protected from damage when you hit the ground.
- It is much easier to drift, in other words, the board can move sideways more easily in order to make better use of a wave.

It is absolutely essential to attach the daggerboard to the mast foot for safety.

The best surfers take the daggerboard right out in breaking surf. Starting without a daggerboard is not so easy, it is true (see p.133) but the pleasure that you experience is all the greater when you do succeed. Riding down the waves without a daggerboard comes very close to real wave-riding.

When the wind reaches about force 5 a storm sail should be used because it is so much easier to pull out of the water in breaking surf.

You should try to find a part of the beach where the wind is not blowing exactly onto the shore. It is easier when the wind is abeam because you can get out beyond the breakers at one attempt. Insert the mast foot firmly into the board while you are on land and pull the sailboard into shallow water. Above all avoid taking the two parts into the water separately. The board would immediately drift away while the sail would be filled by the first wave and probably sink to the bottom.

As soon as you have reached knee-deep water either stand near the board or in the starting position and wait for an appropriate formation of waves. Never set off immediately. This is the moment to keep calm. The crucial factor is that breaking surf consists of waves which not only vary in height but also occur at irregular intervals. A series of higher waves is always followed by a series of smaller waves. You should therefore start at an appropriate moment when you see a low wave approaching. Before you reach that wave you first have to surmount the foam top of the preceding wave, and this will sometimes reach you as a wall of water several feet high. To prevent your board cutting into it and braking your speed too much you must move your weight onto the back foot shortly before reaching the breaker so that the bows of the board lift to it. At the same time ensure that your sail does not get filled along the foot by the mass of water which tumbles over the board. To avoid this you must incline the mast forward at the right moment so that the foot is lifted high. Remember too that your speed will be braked when you force your way through the foam top and lean well back. This is very similar to skiing when you run from a fast, smooth piste into deep snow. Now sail with great determination towards the next wave that is building up. You must reach it before it breaks or all is lost. You will then shoot up the slope of the wave at full speed, and this is a feeling that only sailboarders know because normal surfers have to paddle their way energetically through this phase. Prepare yourself mentally to fly for the first time on your sailboard because you are about to make a tremendous leap. When you are on the crest of the wave ease the sail

Carry the fully assembled surfboard and rig to the water (above). Pull it into deeper water by the mast (centre). Get aboard quickly and get under way before the next wave arrives. If you can, start with the daggerboard removed.

At full speed climb up the wave and over the top with the sail hardened . . .

immediately ease out the sail . . .

slightly and 'take off'. For your first free flight concentrate the centre of gravity of your body over your aft foot in so far as this is possible. Landing is very like skiing again, and you must bend your knees well to absorb the shock. Then harden the sail and get under way again.

After you have sailed over the next wave at the same speed, and have altered course with an elegant jump

tack, you can sit on the board and look back at the breaking surf from seaward for the first time. As you will certainly not be the only one to go into the breakers you can watch the other surfers jumping from here.

When surfing with the waves you must take care that the board does not cut under them. It does happen sometimes so move your weight aft and slow

and vanish behind the wave

The wave now breaks harmlessly.

129

down because, otherwise, the board will bore down even deeper. In the truest sense of the expression you go to diving stations. The easiest method is to luff up if you can because this is the quickest way to bring the board clear. A man who can lift his board clear again with a gybe can consider himself to be a real master.

Try to sail in the trough between two waves and, as your speed is reduced, let yourself be overtaken by the wave. As soon as the stern lifts harden the sail and increase speed.

It is not until you can stay with a high wave in a good breeze and thus really get going that you will realize just how fast a sailboard can move. You could even reach 20—25 knots. The result of this is an effect which has been pure theory until now. Board speed increases so much that the true wind from abeam is overwhelmed. Pressure on the sail ceases and the board now has to be steered with your feet. The centre of gravity of your body has to be brought over the board because it is no longer possible to lean out or hang out on the rig.

If you are surfing in a gentle breeze, use of the sail, coupled with good footwork, becomes important. Alternately sheet the sail in to climb a wave, and let it out and move your weight back to descend, in order to maintain stability and prevent the bow from submerging in the next trough.

Do not leave it too late to think about tacking. Before you start to go about you should try to sail away from the wave a little. You can then go about more easily because you are not hanging at such an angle in front of the wave. You tack over the crest while the wave runs underneath you. Later, when you wish to use a wave to surf back to the beach, search for one which is not too large so that you avoid the risk of damage. The essential point is that you must be as far ahead of the wave as possible when it breaks. In other words, you must be sure to avoid having the mass of breaking water fall on your board so, in good time, take up a course which leads you at an angle safely down the front of the wave. It will then topple over astern of you while the powerful foam top will thrust you forward and, more important, give you enough depth of water to enable you to surf almost to the shore.

Sailboarding Without a Daggerboard

As you know, the daggerboard discourages the board from making leeway. The larger the area of the daggerboard the less leeway the board will make and vice versa.

The amount of leeway made increases as you sail closer to the wind and decreases when you bear away to a broad reach, finally becoming nil when you are on a run. This is why more and more sailboarders can be seen pulling their daggerboards half or completely out when on a run during a race. The object is to reduce the turbulence which is caused by the daggerboard and which slows the surfboard. A possible disadvantage has to be taken into account because it is easy to fall into the water when pulling the daggerboard out due to the fact that the board is much less stable when the daggerboard is removed, and this is particularly the case when the wind is very light.

The time when it becomes really important to sail without a daggerboard, or with it half raised, is when the wind is blowing at force 5 or more because it is then, when you are on the faster points of sailing, reaching and beam reaching, that the danger of capsize falling is always present. The daggerboard then becomes a hindrance on these points of sailing in particular and, in any case, when sailing with the wind free, the amount of leeway made is only minimal. Just reducing the area of the daggerboard, as in the case of the Hawaii or combination daggerboard, considerably discourages the tendency of the board to turn over; if it is removed entirely the board cannot capsize at all. The danger of capsize falling is greatest in waves and we therefore recommend you to sail without a daggerboard, or with one of reduced area when waves are high, and that includes both people who sail in breaking surf and strong wind enthusiasts. Such experts can be seen more and more frequently in winds between force 6 and 8, beating laboriously up to windward and then turning their board round with a quick tack, pulling out their daggerboards, sometimes with the sail lowered, and flying back with the daggerboard hanging over one arm. This is quite an art, but once you have mastered it completely it is by far the most satisfying way of sailboarding. If you intend to start learning how to sail without a daggerboard bear the following in mind:

Starting on a Broad Reach

1. Do not try at all in winds of under force 4.

2. Leave the sail hand free and, with the mast hand grasp the wishbone boom about 12—15in aft of the mast, pulling it over to windward. While the sail is still shaking turn the board a few degrees further to a very broad reaching position.

3. Bend over, pull the daggerboard out of the case with your sail hand and hang it on your wrist by the line or strap attached to it. Then straighten up again and place your front foot about 2in to windward of the mast. Your aft foot should be about a hand's breadth to leeward of the daggerboard slot and about 18in aft of it.

4. Pull the sail well to windward with your mast hand. The sail hand grasps the boom about 3ft further aft. Lean out well to windward and aft as well while you harden the sail.

Altering Course with No Daggerboard

5. The surfboard will accelerate very rapidly without the daggerboard, so be prepared for this. Should the bow show a tendency to turn towards the wind you must both incline the mast forward and also pull it over to windward if you are to get the board to bear away. With the mast raked well over like this harden the sail to make the board bear away. Once it starts to turn away from the wind harden the sail further and the board will continue to bear away.

6. If you wish to sail slightly closer to the wind press the lee side of your sailboard just under the water so that you can use the whole length of the board as a keel, but be careful not to pull the sail over too far to windward or you will find it difficult to bear away again. If there is enough wind it is generally possible to sail a close reach, pointing about 10° closer to the wind than a beam reach.

This small Hawaii daggerboard was named after the island where such photographs are taken.

When the daggerboard is removed, start with the board in a broad reaching position because otherwise it will luff towards the wind. Good legwork is required here.

133

7. A fountain of water may shoot out of the dagger-board slot and spray into your eyes. If you find this too disturbing lean back a little and cover the slot with your toes. The faster that the board sails the less high will the fountain spurt because, at high speeds, only the aft third of the board remains in contact with the water.

Starting in a strong wind. Derk Thijs is pulling his sail until it is set for a run, and inclines his mast to windward.

Running in Force 6 Winds

8. If you are sailing dead before the wind, move your weight far aft so that you can keep the tip of the board above the water, and take the mast aft with you. In a strong wind blowing at force 6 your feet will be about 6in aft of the end of the daggerboard slot. The sail-board will be unbelievably stable when running, even when it is making 18 knots. Four-foot waves are easy to take, and gusts no longer present a problem provided you have inclined the mast far enough aft. Strong gusts, however, have to be

countered by pulling the mast towards you with your mast hand, while the sail hand eases the pressure on the sail. This will keep the centre of effort exactly over the centreline. In the same way as when water-skiing you can alter course by moving the weight of your body to one side and by inclining the mast aft and to the opposite side to that in which you wish to go. It is difficult to sail absolutely dead before a wind that is blowing at over force 6, and tacking downwind is then preferable.

9. The bow of the board lifts ever higher out of the water as speed increases until it hovers about 15—20in above it. In order to get the sailboard to sail even faster depress the bow slightly by moving your weight a little further forward and the board will then plane on a film of air, slamming hard on the waves. Many surfers who enjoy this method of surfing without a daggerboard have made a minor alteration to their equipment. Instead of the cord which is often attached to the daggerboard they use strong ¾ or 1 in woven tape which they attach beneath the batten on top of the daggerboard. When this is used the daggerboard cannot swing about in the wind as it does when a cord is attached to the top, and this cord gets twisted tightly and uncomfortably round your arm. Several boards are now delivered with tape already fitted.

To be able to sail on a run in a force 6—7 wind is hot stuff indeed! The snag is that, unfortunately, you first have to gain a good deal of ground to windward, and that is not so easy in winds of over force 6. When beating to windward there are two very important facts to be remembered:

- You are not a machine and, sooner or later, you will get tired.
- The mast of the sailboard bends considerably under the pressure of so strong a wind.

With regard to the first point, whenever possible you should choose a stretch of water which will give you

Brian Tulley from the USA tears along on a run with his sail full and the daggerboard raised. At such speeds the knees must be well bent to increase stability.

a chance to rest and recover your strength if necessary, preferably at the end of the beat. Relax before taking out the daggerboard and haring back home again downwind.

The fact that the mast bends so much on a close hauled course presents a major problem. The top of the sail does not fill, and the upper six feet begin to shake violently in the strong wind, waving about like a flag and consequently reducing the speed of the sailboard. The solution to this problem is the storm sail which lacks the upper portion of the normal sail that first begins to shake, but which retains all that part that continues to draw. When the wind blows at force 6 or over you will beat to windward faster, and also sail faster on a beam reach if you use a storm sail because the sail area when close hauled is virtually the same as the effective part of the normal sail; only that part at the top which would slow the board is missing. When it comes to sailing downwind the larger sail is always faster because the speed of the true wind is decreased by the high speed of the sailboard sailing through the water and the mast can stand up to the reduced pressure without difficulty.

135

Tandem Surfing

A delightful variation on solo sailboarding is the Tandem, when two people sail on one sailboard. You not only sail faster but, because real team-work and understanding are required, you have to become accustomed to working together, coordinating your efforts smoothly in wind, waves and spray. Tandem sailing can become one of the most enjoyable ways of sailing over the water.

The Tandem is also useful for instructional purposes in light airs, and is used by some schools. The pupil stands forward and aft alternately, while his instructor steers the sailboard. This gives the beginner the opportunity both to see and to put into practice, while sailing through the water, all those skills which he would perhaps only learn after falling into the water many times were he sailing alone on his sailboard.

In the same way as with a one-man sailboard, the method of altering course depends on altering the position of the centre of effort of the sails in relation to the centre of lateral resistance, but now the effect of the two sails has to be balanced. The Tandem has two sails, and therefore two independent centres of effort which act in relation to the daggerboard. The forward sail is responsible for bearing away while the aft sail deals with luffing up. The Tandem, then, is a two-man board with no helmsman, both partners being equally responsible for controlling the board.

You have to be completely agreed over every action because if the sails are set wrongly the effect of one sail can completely cancel out the effect of the other sail. If the forward sail is set so that the centre of effort moves aft while the aft sail is moving it forward the effects will cancel each other out, but the airflow over both sails will be affected for the worse and that results in reduced efficiency.

When you react to a change in the wind direction you have to alter your previous habits slightly. As an example, if you wish to luff do not incline the mast well aft immediately because all that is required is for the aft man to harden his sail slightly.

Altering course, going about and gybing are especially good ways of finding out how well the two Tandem sailors cooperate, and will show how much control they have over their sailboard and gear.

If you wish to go about you start in the usual way by inclining the masts well aft. This causes the board to point up high into the wind. The forward man then releases the pressure on his sail, and only the aft sail is hardened fully. To do this the aft man pulls his sail well back over the centreline. As soon as the board is head to wind, or perhaps slightly earlier, the forward man can help the sailboard to turn by thrusting his boom back against the wind. The next stage is the responsibility of the forward man alone. He must be the first to step round the mast, and will then immediately bear away hard while the man aft completes his tack.

A Tandem is extremely useful for instruction. Windglider are most experienced manufacturers of tandems.

When you want to bear away and sail the Tandem on a run, the aft man must ease out his sail completely until the board is on its new course, while the forward man bears away. The former will then be busy again because, when the wind is free, pressure on the aft sail must be maintained continuously if the sailboard is to remain on course.

Once you have borne away onto a run you can gybe. As soon as both partners have swung their sails round forward of the masts the aft man must immediately harden his sail firmly so as to encourage the board to luff up, while the forward man keeps his sail empty and does not harden it until the Tandem has started to gather way. Gybing in stronger winds is always a risky affair because neither partner must let his sail touch the water. The slightest contact with it will lead to breakage because the other sail is still driving the board forwards.

The most important point to remember is that if one partner falls or lets his sail drop the other must react instantaneously. If the board is not immediately brought to a complete halt falls can be very dangerous, due to the exhilarating speed of the Tandem.

Notes on the Tandem Surfboard

The Windglider-Tandem was developed in 1974 by Fred Ostermann and is constructed of fibreglass by the same method as the Windglider. Length 21 ft 4 in beam 2 ft 3½ in, weight 108 lbs.

Car top transport

Possible, if a very strong roof rack is used. Do not forget to tie on a red flag!

Sail arrangement

Two Windglider rigs are used and are stepped in such a way that they can be tacked and gybed without touching each other. If one man falls overboard the Tandem can be sailed by the remaining man alone because there is a third mast step amidships, forward of the daggerboard case.

Method of steering

There are many techniques unique to sailboarding on a Tandem. The forward partner can only bear away while the aft man can only luff. Rôles are divided in the same way when tacking and gybing.

Speed

About 20—30% faster than a one-man sailboard, estimated by direct comparison.

Behaviour in waves

Considerably more stable than any one-man sailboard, and therefore also easier for beginners to balance on. On the other hand tacking and gybing are more difficult in strong winds because the partners have to work with complete mutual understanding.

Strong wind limit

Appears to be unlimited as the forward partner can get the board under way without the problem of luffing up. When using flat storm sails it should be able to fly in force 8 — 9 winds.

Windsurfer rig

Can be used purely for fun, if fitted with the Windglider universal joint. Not allowed, however, in official Tandem class racing.

Surfing Behind a Power Boat

Surfing behind a power boat is an alternative for those who are enthusiastic sailboarders and also like to be able to use their boards when there is no wind. You then stand on the board and are towed behind the power boat as if you were on an enormous water-ski. Surfing like this is not only an excellent way of practising getting your balance for sailboarding but also has a good deal in common with water-skiing. Experienced water-skiers are surprised at the completely different feeling under way. At higher speeds, in particular, you must stand well forward, not only because the resistance of the surfboard would become too great if it were trimmed at too sharp an angle, but because it can be steered more effectively with the weight further forward. Good surfers run up and down the much longer sailboard as if they were on a fixed platform.

As to technique, it is better to start sitting down and not to stand until the boat has gathered way. The power boat should not go too slowly because surfing then becomes more difficult than when you are moving fast.

Derk Thijs surfing under tow. The faster the board travels, the further forward weight should be placed on the board.

140

It is easiest to stay inside the boat's quarter waves, surfing over the wake which is churned up by the propeller. When you decide to cross over the quarter waves remember to move your weight aft before crossing them, and then run forward when you are on the crest of the wave. At the same time let the board slide sideways so that the bow does not cut under the water. After a few hours of practice you can do a slalom and run at very acute angles from one side to the other.

Above about 20 mph an impressive fountain of water shoots up through the daggerboard slot, and it is therefore best to tape over the underwater side of the slot.

Explanation of Some of the More Important Terms Used

WIND

Calm:	no wind or very light airs
Freshening wind:	the wind becomes stronger
Gust:	a sudden increase in wind speed
Fresh wind:	force 5, 17—21 knots
Strong wind:	force 6, 22—27 knots
Backing wind:	the direction of the wind changes in an anti-clockwise direction
Veering wind:	the wind direction changes in a clockwise direction
Heading wind:	the wind direction changes and comes from further forward at a more acute angle to the course being sailed
Freeing wind:	the wind direction changes and comes from further aft
Fluky wind:	the direction of the wind alters continuously
True wind:	the actual wind that strikes a surfboard which is not moving forwards
Board speed:	the speed of the board through the water, giving rise to a head wind
Apparent wind:	the wind which arises when the true wind is combined with the wind due to board speed. The apparent wind is used to sail the board, and is the wind felt when the sailboarder sails through the water
Offshore wind:	wind which blows from the land to the water
Onshore wind:	wind which blows from the water to the land
Windward:	the side which is nearer the wind
Leeward:	the side which is further from the wind

WATER

Breaking waves:	the crests of the waves curl over and break (white horses)
Choppy seas:	short steep seas which do not all move in the same direction
Swell:	long seas which are not due to the wind of the moment
Breaking surf:	waves which break on approaching the shore or shallow water
Current and tidal stream:	horizontal movement of water. Currents often flow in only one direction, or may alter direction due to natural causes such as the wind; tidal streams change direction regularly in response to the rise and fall of the tide
Following seas:	seas overtaking the board from astern
Cross seas:	waves which approach the board from abeam
Head sea:	waves which approach the board from ahead

POINTS OF SAILING

Running:	the wind blows from astern
Broad reach:	the wind blows from over the quarter at an angle of between approximately 100° and 170° to the centreline
Beam reach:	the wind blows from abeam at approximately 90° to the centreline
Close reach:	the wind blows from slightly forward of abeam
Close hauled:	the board sails as close to the wind as possible, and the wind comes from ahead at an angle of about 45° to the centreline
Beating:	sailing a zig-zag course to windward close hauled on alternate tacks

ALTERING COURSE

Luff up:	change direction to sail a course closer to the wind
Bear away:	change direction to sail a course further from the wind
Tacking, or going about:	turning from one tack to the other with the bows passing through the eye of the wind
Gybing:	turning from one tack to the other with the stern passing through the wind

SAIL HANDLING

Harden:	bring the sail closer to the body with the sail hand
Ease:	easing wind pressure on the sail by stretching the sail hand to let the sail out further
Backing the sail:	holding the sail pressed back against the wind in the direction in which the board is moving

THE SURFBOARD

Port:	the left hand side of the board when looking forward
Starboard:	the right side when looking forward
Port tack:	the wind is blowing from port (port tack gives way to starboard tack)
Starboard tack:	the wind strikes the starboard side first
Stern:	the back end of the surfboard
Aft:	towards the stern
Bow:	the point at the front of the surfboard
Forward:	towards the bow
Centreline or fore-and-aft line:	the imaginary line between the bow and stern of the board
Abeam:	at right angles to the centreline of the board
Centre of effort, CE:	the total aerodynamic force that results from the varying pressures to windward and leeward of a sail is said to act through the centre of effort of the sail
Underwater body:	all that part of the surfboard or boat, together with daggerboard and fin, which are beneath the water
Centre of lateral resistance, CLR:	the imaginary point in the underwater body through which the forces of lateral resistance act. This centre is on the axis about which the board pivots
Leeway:	leeway is the angle between the direction in which the board is pointing and the track which it sails
Drift:	movement over the ground due to currents or tidal streams, also movement through the water when an object is blown to leeward by the wind
Sheer or rocker:	the upward curve of the board along its length
Chine:	the side of the board

Beaufort Scale: the strength of the wind and the state of the sea

Scale No.	Knots	Km.p.h	State of the Sea
0 = calm	under 1	under 1	like a mirror
1 = light air	1–3	1–5	ripples
2 = light breeze	4–6	6–11	small wavelets
3 = gentle breeze	7–10	12–19	large wavelets, crests begin to break
4 = moderate breeze	11–16	20–28	small waves, fairly frequent white horses
5 = fresh breeze	17–21	29–38	moderate and longer waves, many white horses
6 = strong breeze	22–27	39–49	large waves, extensive white foam crests
7 = near gale	28–33	50–61	sea heaps up, white foam blown in streaks
8 = gale	34–40	62–74	moderately high waves, spindrift, foam in well-marked streaks
9 = strong gale	41–47	75–88	high waves, dense streaks of foam, wave crests beginning to tumble
10 = storm	48–55	89–102	very high waves with long over-hanging crests
11 = violent storm	56–63	103–117	exceptionally high waves
12 = hurricane	over 63	over 117	sea completely white with driving spray